8

The

The Mother of Christ

Caryll Houselander

Sheed and Ward
London

Publisher's Note

Caryll Houselander wrote numerous articles for journals such as the *Messenger of the Sacred Heart*, the *Tablet*, *Integrity*, in addition to the half-dozen or so books published before her death in 1954. A selection of these, mostly written just after the war, on themes that will be familiar to her readers, are here brought together for the first time in book form.

Contents

The Mother of Christ

The Mother of Christ

MAGNIFICAT

Several times recently I have read detailed plans for proposed 'Schools of Mothercraft'. How to prepare the baby's food, wash his clothes, and him, how to look after his health, from birth to little boyhood, or little girlhood, and so on.

Of course it is all a very good idea, but when I put down the syllabus and shut my eyes and think about the world that this baby is going to be born into, and what he is going to be born for, and how much further than up to little boyhood or little girlhood his mother's love must carry him, I begin to wonder. Then when I think of how young his mother is likely to be if he is the first child, I wonder still more seriously, because I am more and more sure that the school of mothercraft, good though it is, will not be able to give her anything essential to help her: in fact she will need something else altogether even to give real meaning to the expression of love that lies in the daily routine of washing and feeding and nursing the baby.

She will need the descent of the Holy Ghost, all the gifts and fruits of the spirit, beginning as they do with wisdom and understanding.

We have all received those gifts in confirmation, but we do not all know how to use them. The girl with her first baby needs to learn that more than anything else and she cannot learn from anyone else so well as from Mary, the mother of the Word Incarnate, who conceived by the Holy Ghost.

Our Lady has so much in common with the mothers of

first babies, perhaps especially with those of our day. She too was very young when her son was born, she too through unexpected circumstances was faced with the problem of having no home for her new baby, of being turned away from house after house. She even went from door to door seeking in vain for somewhere to give birth to him, and in the end had to go to a stable. She learnt her mothercraft from the child himself.

It is in the relationship of Christ with his mother that we can see God's design for the relationship of every mother and child.

Our lady knew perfectly well what kind of a world it was into which Christ was to be born. It is strange that she did, for her own life had been sheltered enough, lived in Nazareth, an out-of-the-way village, lying in a ring of hills like the hollow in a chalice. Her future too was mapped out on simple, happy lines. She was betrothed to Joseph, her home was ready for her, it seemed almost certain that in front of her lay a lifetime of uneventful but serene happiness.

The first shadow to fall was the shadow of the angel's wing when Gabriel came to tell her that she was to be the mother of Christ.

What faith in her son's vocation would be demanded of her! What baffling things she would have to face! The slaughter of the innocents and Christ the innocent cause of it, the flight from Herod, the life in exile, and the child being hunted all his life long, his fasting, so much against the grain for a mother, his choice to be homeless, after all the years that she had longed for and waited for their home together. The pitiless demands made on him by strangers, put before her own claim, the selfishness of the people's approach to him, the ingratitude shown to him, even hatred of him and fear, the misunderstanding of his closest friends. At the end there was not even one voice to speak aloud for him. And then the public death, and that burial of his, rushed through against time and in a borrowed tomb.

What wisdom was it, what knowledge, that made our Lady able to accept these things and say 'Be it done unto me according to thy word' with so whole a will? It was her understanding of two great truths:

That her child was God's child.
That her child was Christ.

Every mother after her has to realise these same truths, and to learn their meaning literally by heart, if she is to be true to God's design of motherhood. For every child born is God's child first, even before he is his mother's, and every christian born is born to be 'another Christ'.

The first of these two truths makes it easier to bear the second; it means that God loves the child even more than his mother does. He loves with the love of creator and father and mother. He loves with absolute knowledge and absolute power. Nothing can befall the child without the Heavenly Father's knowledge and consent, and he can bring good even out of the evil which we ourselves bring upon our children. From the first breath the child draws to the last he is in the hands of infinite, eternal love.

The second truth, though a blessed one in fact, is a hard one for the mother's nature. For while the first has its comfort, something in it of return, going back, to safety, to home, this being another Christ means going out alone, to hardship, danger and perhaps to death.

Our Lady was not fifteen years old at the time of the Annunciation. What was the secret which enabled her to translate all this suffering into joy? It was the secret of the twofold love, which our Lord tells us is one and the same: the love of God and the love of man.

It is in the *Magnificat*, that wonderful expression of joy, with which she answered the greeting of her cousin Elizabeth, that our Lady shows this twofold love, and shows how the love of God and the love of man was interlocked in her mind.

If you think of her circumstances at the time, it is

astonishing that she should have loved the world as she did, and that she should have felt its sorrows so intensely.

She was a country girl who had spent all her life between the temple and a sheltered home. She lived frugally, but she had had no personal experience of want, let alone hunger. She knew nothing of life in the cities, there was nothing, we would have thought, to fire her imagination with the injustice of the world, nothing to lay its sorrows upon her heart, nothing at all to make any of it a reality to her. Yet clearly, after God, it was the supreme reality.

Compare her attitude with that of a girl of today, brought up in a convent school and a good home. The world's agony is publicised, exploited, advertised, commercialised. It is thrown in front of our eyes on the screen, it is front page news, it is published everywhere in photographs, it is shouted into our ears in every propaganda speech, it is broadcast by the BBC. We cannot possibly avoid knowing it, do what we will. Moreover it is seared and carved on the bodies of the people we meet in the street. Even in London, there are districts where one is abashed by the numbers of mutilated people whom one meets in a single hour. The words of prophecy seem to smite one like a blow: 'Is it nothing to you, all you who pass by?'

How many of us, young or old, really take it to heart, really care at all? How many think about it? Face it squarely, and do not try to forget it? How many ask themselves honestly,

'What is the root cause of all this?'
'Is there a remedy?'
'What effect on it does my life have?'
'Have I done anything at all to ease one tittle of it?'
'Have I added to it by even the weight of a feather?'
'What is the effect of my indifference?'
'Do I want to carry my full share of the weight of the world's sorrow?'

To take the simplest test of sincerity, how many deplore, shall we say, Belsen Camp? How many who would impose a rigorous diet on themselves in order to slim, would fast for a single day in reparation for the sin that is starving Europe? Or how many even of those who do believe in reparation would refrain from grumbling about ration cards and clothing coupons?

Now how many mothers today so love the world that they would honestly rejoice if their child turned his back on human respect, worldly success, wealth and on the compromise that we love to flatter by the name of common sense, and chose instead hardship, poverty, contempt for the sake of his fellow men, and not even for the sake of his own countrymen, but for the people of a foreign country, and for their children?

Our Lady had just such a love for the world—for us! It was that love which made her able to rejoice that her child had come to save the world, cost him and cost her what it must. Her imagination did seize upon our suffering, her heart did go out across the ages to us. Not the politicians of today, but the peasant girl of two thousand years ago knew the root and the remedy for our sorrow.

She rejoiced, not first of all because she was to be the mother of God, not first of all in the sweetness of having a child of her own, but because her child was coming into the world to be light, humility, gentleness, justice, for the healing of the wounds of pride; because he who now lived in her was the world's life, and his love would prevail from generation to generation.

She loved man, and she loved God. One thing which may have helped her to love the human race was the scripture which she learned in the temple. She would have pored over the prophecies foretelling the passion, and her sensitive mind would have learnt suffering by heart, from the vision of the wounds from head to foot and the bowed thorn-crowned head of uncreated love.

Her kinsmen covered their faces and trembled before God. There was no want of wonder and awe in Mary, but her adoration pierced the veil of the temple, she discovered the heart of God. Because she discovered his heart in her own, she knew his tenderness as well as his might. She knew the mother in him as well as the father. She rejoiced in his care for the little and weak. 'He hath put down the mighty from their seats and hath exalted the humble'.

The love of God and the love of man, this is the twofold love that should inform the mind and will of all motherhood. It was this which was the secret of our Lady's serenity.

Yet it remains puzzling that she should love *us*. It is not so easy for us to love one another. I am afraid that to many of us the question 'why did God create my neighbour?' is an even more puzzling one than 'why did God create me?' It is always astonishing, even humbling, to find oneself loved, even when it is by someone who has the fellow-feeling that comes from being a fellow sinner. But our Lady was sinless, and her vision was clear. Why then did she, seeing us as we are, seeing us now, knowing us, love us?

I think that the answer was this: it was because she saw the reality. It is Christ whom she loves in us. In the life of Christ in her own being, the life of the world was quickened. She was pregnant with the Christ life of the whole world. No one of us would ever be a stranger to her in a strange land: to her every one of us would be her only child.

In the fusion of these two loves, the love of God and the love of man, there is another love which is still the same, but to her the most natural and the tenderest of all, the love of Christ who is both God and man.

MY FATHER'S BUSINESS

There is a psychological as well as a physical travail. It is not only once that a mother must give birth to her child, but over and over again, and each time with a new sense of separation, a new mental travail. Before her child was born, he was part of her, his heartbeat in her heartbeat, his life was simply her life, his birth was the first separation. Now he is outside her with his own separate life, but he is still dependent on her to sustain his life. Soon, however, the second separation comes, the infant is weaned, he has become a baby, and next the baby must be set on his feet and taught to walk away. He in his turn must give place to the little boy, the little boy to the schoolboy, the schoolboy to the adolescent, finally the adolescent to the man.

At each step well-meaning friends will tell the mother that the child is passing through 'a difficult phase', but is only when he becomes that strange, baffling thing an adolescent that she really will believe in this 'difficult phase'.

Every step in his growth has been a preparation for this one, at each step there has been a new challenge to the mother's courage. This means that if she has any of our Lady's wisdom she will have called on God, the Heavenly Father, again and again in breathless trust, and so she will have experienced his tender care for her child again and again, and have learnt to trust him.

Nothing teaches us to pray so surely as loving someone else, and if that someone is our child this is more than ever true, for to a mother her child seems so frail, so small to set out into the world on his first unsteady footsteps. All the winds seem to be sharpened against him, all the storms to beat upon him, his path is beset with stones, the powers of evil are mobilised against him, all the storms too—or so his mother thinks, for she measures his frailty by her protective love.

Only the fatherhood of God, dared by faith, known by the experience that comes from faith, can give to the mother of a small child the strong and tranquil heart which is the beginning of his own courage through life.

It is all too easy for the mother who forgets God's father-hood to let a habit of anxiety and fear become an obsession, and then the ever-recurring note in her heart, in her thoughts, in her words, will be 'Take Care!' Take care you don't fall down, take care you don't get wet, take care you don't catch cold, take care you don't get too hot, and so on until at last the child accepts the continual suggestion of danger, and very likely the habit of fear instilled in him remains to cripple his whole life.

Even if the mother tries to conceal her anxiety and restrains the outward expression of it, the child will sense it. The peace of heart which is to be the rock on which his own courage is founded must be the real thing, *real* trust in God. No child has ever yet found security in a sham. On the mother's courage for the little boy his courage as a man will largely depend. The mother's courage is one thing only, trust in God.

The other attitude, anxiety, or as it can more truly be called, mistrust in God, sometimes makes a mother try to keep her child dependent on her. She wants him to go on being a baby, always within the reach of her protecting hands, always bound to her by chains of helplessness. All too often she succeeds, and long after she is dead or circumstances have forced them apart, the crippled man who is still her baby goes through life looking for a mother on whom he can lay the burden of his own responsibilities, finding her in every woman who comes into his life.

Because of her immaculate conception our Lady could not know the physical travail of childbirth that other women do, but that yet more searching psychological travail she knew better than any other woman can ever do.

If it demands courage and trust for any woman to set her little son on his feet and to fold her hands in prayer while he takes his first steps, how much more must it have demanded from the mother of Christ?

When she taught her son his first footsteps, she knew that she was setting his feet on the road to Calvary; every step that he took was a step nearer to the cross. She must have

seen symbol upon symbol of his passion even in his little
boy-life, signs of his passion but also of the glory he was to
be in the heart of man. Imagine her thoughts when she
taught him, the light of the world, to light a candle! Or
when they watched the birds together would he, the bread
of life, have noticed that the bird carried a morsel in its beak
to feed its little ones? Or she, that the spread wings in flight
to the nest are cruciform?

Perhaps, like many mothers, she marked her son's height
on the wall: she knew that every inch that he grew was an
inch closer to the size of the cross.

Even in the very little that is said about our Lady in the
gospels, there is evidence that she brought the utmost trust
in God and courage to Christ's growing from babyhood to
boyhood. That travail of the heart bravely born had
prepared her for his adolescence, and when it came her heart
answered as her words had answered in Nazareth, 'Be it done
unto me according to your word'.

There is a detail in St Luke's story of the loss of the child
Jesus at twelve years old which proves that, even at that
young age, he was already used to his freedom and independence. For had it not been quite an ordinary thing for him
to go off on his own, and devote hours of his time to people
outside his immediate family circle, our Lady would not have
gone a whole day's journey without looking for him, or have
taken it for granted, as she did, that he was with some of
their fellow travellers. That is what actually happened.

The whole incident of the three days' loss and the finding
of the child in the temple pours a flood of light on the crisis
of adolescence, and the inner meaning of so much that is
baffling.

First there is the sense of loss that is experienced by the
mother of every normal child when he is beginning to grow
up. For now that the boy is to become a man there must
inevitably be a reorientation of his whole life, a going forth,
a going out to new friends, new emotions, new ideas, new

loves, to his own work in the world, ultimately to the founding of his own home and his own family.

For the mother this is the hardest travail of all. It is now that she has to say 'He must increase; but I must decrease', and now more than ever before must the mother remember that her son is 'another Christ', that he has come into this world to do his Father's will. He belongs to God and because he belongs to God he belongs to all humanity; the human race is his family and he has to grow up in order that he may give his quota of love and service.

Just in the measure in which she recognises Christ in her son, the mother will be true or untrue in the eyes of God to her mysterious vocation of motherhood.

What does it mean, this being 'another Christ'? It means that we live in Christ, that he lives in us, his life is in us, as the grapes are on the branches of the vine. He lives our life in us, whatever our way in life may be. Each one of us has a vocation that comes before all others, to give Christ's redeeming love to the world.

There are as many ways of being 'another Christ' as there are individuals in the world. Of course it does not mean that every christian could or should try to copy all the outward circumstances of Christ's earthly life (though all share fully in its spirit) but each lives some one aspect of Christ's life. Some live more than one aspect during their lifetime; some are sanctified by his childhood, some by the solitude and fasting in the wilderness, others live the fiercely hard life of his temptations, others the active public life, and yet others drain the cup of his passion. But all, and this is an unimaginable mercy, live his risen life, for that is what christianity is, the risen life of Christ being lived in all his members in his mystical body.

Almost certainly a child forms his own unconscious but immensely effective valuation of himself by his mother's recognition or lack of recognition of the Christ in him.

To make my meaning clearer here is an example from

life. The child of poor, working parents was born with a disease of the bones which was incurable, and made him quite dependent on other people for everything. His mother saw the likeness in his life to the life of the host. Therefore he grew up realising that he shared in the reparation being continually made by our Lord in the tabernacle and on the altar, by the littleness, the helplessness, the dependence on creatures, the hiddenness, the laid-asideness of the sacred host. The little boy knew that he was taking his part in the world's healing, that he was comforting, redeeming, bringing light just as truly as priests, scientists, teachers and doctors, that he was fighting for the spirit of man just as really as any soldier on the battlefield. In that boy's family, and in himself, there was no sense of frustration, no self-pity, but there was joy, such as many people with good health, and all that this world can give, cannot begin to imagine.

When at the end of her three days' search, our Lady found our Lord in the temple she, who always acted for all humanity as much as for herself, asked him the question which sooner or later forms in the heart of every mother: 'Son, why hast thou done so to us?' and his answer rings down the ages for all the children of God: 'Did you not know that I must be about my Father's business?'

Of course our Lord had always been about his Father's business, but twelve years old is a Jewish boy's coming of age, and he was speaking for every boy who is facing the world with his first realisation of himself as a man in it. He was facing his vocation as himself in the world, Christ in the world, just as every christian boy has to do when he is adolescent.

The word 'vocation' may bring a smile of irony today, when so few are free to choose work which seems to them to be anything that they are called to, or through which they can really express the good that is in them, but even when a boy cannot choose exactly what life he will lead, he can choose exactly how he will lead his life.

He can comfort himself by the certainty that, if there is no sin in it, the work he must do is the work God wants him to do, if not for ever, at least for today. If he is in this particular workroom or office it is because here it is that Christ wishes to be today. If he is among these particular people it is because it is to these particular people that Christ wants to give his love today. If he has this particular work to do, it is because Christ wants that particular job done in his way. Because these facts are true, it is a more glorious and a more apostolic thing for that boy to do that job, in the name and the power of Christ, than (imagining this to be possible) to convert the whole of Asia in his own name and power. To do the ordinary work of the world with Christ's integrity is to be about the Father's business.

It sounds very banal, very obvious indeed, to say that a christian must choose, as the minimum, truth, honesty, justice, humility, kindness; in every detail of his daily life he must make Christ's values his values; he must put the good quality of his work before profit, gentleness before self-advancement, kindness before self-interest, justice before the line of least resistance . . . but it only sounds banal and obvious to those who have not tried to earn their living in an office or factory or shop, who have taken no part in any professional life, who have not lived among the great multitude of good natured people who regard loyalty to God as a somewhat indecent manifestation of mental deficiency, or worked for an employer whose only consideration is money. Those who have know that this simple, basic christianity, professed by almost everyone, practised by almost no one, involves heroism.

At first glance it seems surprising that our Lord should have gone back to Nazareth with Mary and Joseph and, as the gospel tells us, obeyed them, after they had found him in the temple. It looks almost like an anti-climax. After his dramatic disappearance, and that ringing declaration of independence one might expect to read that he went on into the world, taking farewell of his parents, instead of which we read this almost baffling statement: 'And he went down with them, and came to Nazareth, and was subject to them'.

It was not for a few months, but for over twenty years that Christ remained in Nazareth and was obedient. This is even more surprising in view of the fact that his parents did not understand his meaning in what he had said to them in the temple. We are told baldly 'They understood not the word that he spoke to them'.

Twenty years still unknown, working as an artisan, living in obedience, the son of the house, in a remote hamlet! Does not this prove that Christ recognised the ordinary work of the world, earning his daily bread, as his Father's business?

And his obedience to Mary, he the boy who had come of age and 'set his face steadfastly towards Jerusalem', does not this prove how entirely he could trust his mother's love of God, that he knew that no command of hers, no least wish of hers, could ever be other than perfectly one with God's will?

It was not necessary for her to understand his strange words to her in the temple, between them there was something more than superficial understanding—real communion. When he was still in her womb she had rejoiced because her child was given, not for her personal satisfaction, Heaven though he was to her, but for the world's redemption. She knew that without understanding his words she could trust his acts.

Other mothers, seeing such singular gifts as Christ must have had, such gifts of mind and body, such skill and such brilliance of thought, would surely have fretted if such a son had not shown more ambition, had not made a name for himself, why be a humble carpenter? For example, with his ability, and his imagination, he could become famous as a wood sculptor. Another mother would have complained that so brilliant a boy could surely better himself and her family fortune at the same time! Had she not seen with her own eyes that even the proud Rabbis were awed and silenced by his uncanny wisdom? Was it not the duty of such a son to provide a little comfort for his mother's old age?

But for Mary of Nazareth, it was enough that her son was about his Father's work. That is what he had said and his word was good enough for her. She knew that if he chose to be a poor working boy, absorbed in his trade, putting all that was in him into his humble job as an ordinary woodworker, if he was content and proud to bring home his labourer's pay towards their daily bread, then most certainly that was God's work. 'He has put down the mighty from their seats and hath exalted the humble.'

He obeyed her because he could trust her, because she never resisted the Holy Spirit by whom she had conceived him, because she was passionately devoted to the will of God, because she loved the world. Her values were his values. Their own miracle went on, and it went on as mysteriously and secretly as a pure bright stream running underground. Just as Christ had received God's love from Mary in his infancy, now he did God's will in the little acts of obedience that filled the loveliness of their lives between the loss in the temple and the temptation in the wilderness.

That which had been the secret of her strength from the beginning was the secret of the communion between them now. The love of God and the love of man, the twofold love which made them one even more than the blood-relationship of mother and son. He knew that if she did not understand his words in the temple, she had a far deeper kind of understanding which made her keep all his words in her heart. She understood his utter devotion to his Father's will because she shared it. She understood his illimitable compassion for the world, because she knew it in herself.

Her Christ must be Christ to the world. For that he must grow up, for that he must be given, given in the sawing and planing and smoothing of the sweet long planks of wood in Nazareth, given in his flowering and dying on the wood of the cross on Calvary. For this she too was given, given all through the years in the secret courage of her love, in every detail of their life together. For this she had borne him and taken him from her breast, for this she had put him down from her arms and set him on his feet, for this all generations shall call her blessed.

In the gradual of the mass on the feast of the most Holy Heart of Mary, the church puts these words into our Lady's mouth. They are the perfect prayer for every mother of a child who is growing up:

My heart is ready, O God of my heart, my heart is ready that I may do thy will, with a great heart and a willing mind.

THE HOUSE ON THE ROCK

That which stands out in the divine infancy is how completely dependent the infant Jesus was on his mother for his life and for everything. Born as he was far from home, in a strange town, in a cold rough stable, he had not even those comforts which most babies have, even the poorest, and which in fact his mother had prepared for him: his cradle, for example, waiting for him in the little home in Nazareth and destined to wait there, empty, until he had outgrown it.

In Bethlehem, in the desert, what had Christ to sustain his life but his mother? She was so much more to him than one who wrapped him in swaddling bands, one who rocked his cradle and prepared his food. She was herself, his warmth, his cradle, his food.

The mother is the trustee of God's love to her baby. Yes, but she is even more than that, she *is* God's love to him. Giving her to him, God gives himself.

What a mystery it is, as unimaginable as the blessed sacrament, that Christ as man was first given God in this world by a woman!

Motherhood is an intimate contemplation of God. How

could anyone learn more of him than she does who learns, not from books and sermons and meditations, not from the secret manifestations or from the blindness and uncertainty of human thought, but from the secret manifestations of God's love in her own being?

Many people think that in order to be contemplative we must be unnatural, either unnatural or oriental, best of all an unnatural oriental. Those who think in this way have not yet pondered the showing forth of God in all that is closest at hand in everything that is around us, above all in human nature.

Human nature is made in God's image. That image burns in its dark heart as the distant star burns in a deep well far below it.

In so far as human beings retain or recover the primitive purity of their human nature they learn the secrets of God from their own hearts.

No man can see God. If we could hold up a mirror to catch one ray of his light, we would be blinded by its glory. But the glory of God is more truly reflected in our dark human nature than in the brightest silver, and we are not blinded, our own darkness is a sufficient cloud: 'The light shone in darkness and the darkness did not comprehend it'.

We learn God slowly, quietly, in great joy, and sometimes in great sadness, through our own deepest and simplest experience. We know the father and mother in God by being fathers and mothers, we come to know his care for us by our care for one wholly dear to us and wholly dependent on us.

God made the beauty of the created world for us. He sowed the fields with bread, but this was not enough for his love: he must *be* our bread. He took his simplest lowliest gift and changed it to himself, that he himself might be our food. Can anyone know the God who gave us himself in the blessed sacrament better than the mother who feeds her child at her breast?

A baby and a tiny child receives God through his mother.

He does so unconsciously of course, taking everything for granted. His attitude to her is subjective, an innocent selfishness; he is aware of her simply as a part of himself, his bodily comfort, warmth, food, and sleep.

His first glimmering of understanding of her as a separate being is of her in things, things which are outside himself, but are *for* him, and which he will very soon assimilate into himself. She is a glass of milk, a sugar biscuit, a warm cot, a night light.

His awareness of her as another person increases as his need for someone other than himself to reassure and comfort him increases, and he comes to know her more and more, and in different ways, as his own mind begins to wake, and he grows conscious of himself as a human being, with other hungers and thirsts than those of a little animal.

Now she is a reassuring voice, a hand that can be reached out to and found in the darkness, the coolness on his forehead in fevers of childhood. She is all beauty too, a voice telling the stories of Hans Andersen, the texture and fold of a certain unforgettable dress, a unique fragrance, illimitable stillness. By the time he comes to the age of reason all these things and more gather together and merge into one idea, which includes everything—Home.

To a young child home stands for God. In it he learns to see and touch the gifts of God. If his mother is wise she will make his home beautiful. She will copy the world's creator and make a tiny new Eden. She will bring in flowers and give the child animals and feed the birds. The food on the table will be clean and simple and good. It will not only taste nice, it will look nice. From all this the child will learn naturally that God did not make the hideous travesty that we have made of created things.

It is in his home that the child should assimilate the teaching of the Sermon on the Mount, not as if it were being drilled into his brain by words, but as if he were breathing it into his whole being like the air.

'Consider the lilies of the field' does not only mean enjoy their brief loveliness, but discover the lyrical quality of the love that has strewn them under your feet.

The ordering of time, which seems so simple, really requires great skill and energy from the mother. It has tremendous importance, above all if it is related (as it obviously should be) to the rhythm of day and night and is interwoven with prayer.

The child should wake with the singing of birds (and they sing in the cities as well as in the woods). Give his heart to God, when light is young, play for long hours when the world is awake and lively. He should form habits of regular hunger and thirst, so that food and hunger come together, and his grace is a real thanking. With twilight there should come stillness in the house and he should be lit to bed by the stars.

From such ordering of time he will learn unconsciously, though it may be many years before he thinks this out, that he is not part of the chaos that man has made of this world, with its fearful abuse of time, but part of an ordered plan of love.

I think that anyone, certainly any woman, who had followed our Lord about the countryside and heard him teaching the people, could have guessed a lot about his boyhood's home. The images that he used show intimate knowledge of things which he could only have become familiar with as a child at home, certainly not as a wandering preacher.

It is not fantastic to presume that since by his own will Christ as an infant received God's love through Mary, since it was she who clothed him, fed him, bathed him, taught him to walk and to speak, it was she too who first took him out into the fields to see the grass and the wild flowers and bade him keep as still as a mouse to watch the sparrows.

If we may guess that he was thinking of his mother when he began telling of his Father's love and how it is shown through flowers and birds, we may certainly be sure that he was thinking of her when he spoke of the mothering hen gathering her chickens under her wings.

The images that he used evoke picture after picture of his home life. As you listen to him, you can almost see the grave little boy watching his mother with the absorbed interest that children always bring to skilled work beautifully done, watching her cook and sweep and bake, put the oil in the lamps, light the candles and bottle the wine.

Listen to some of his images: you cannot mend an old garment with a new piece of cloth. (How many men would know that?) You cannot put new wine into old bottles. Then cleansing of cups and platters, which is just washing up. The candle set high to light the whole room, the sweeping of the house, the annoyance of rust and the inevitable moth! Children clamouring for food and the parents who know how to give good gifts to their children. The oil for the lamps and the leaven put into the bread for the baking.

There is one more image about home, one that brings us sharply up to the modern world. This is the two houses, one built on a rock and the other on sand.

By the time a child comes to the age of reason home, with all its order, happiness and beauty, means just one thing to him: certainty. In this respect home is to him precisely what God is to him, it is safe and certain and permanent, not simply because it is a house with four walls and a roof, but because it is built on the rock of love, his parents' love for God, and for one another, and for him. If a mother shatters her child's faith in her at this moment in his life, she shatters his faith in God.

Trust is natural to a child. How could it be otherwise, he has never had any reason to doubt? The taking for granted which is characteristic of children is the unopened bud of the sublime trust in God which is characteristic of the saints. But if a child is betrayed by his mother who, remember, is God to him, trust will no longer be a natural instinct in him, but cynicism will be. He may possibly learn to trust God again some day, but his way will be bitter and hard, a passage through doubt, a pathway strewn with sharp stones.

One of the complaints illogically but continually levelled at God today, is that innocent little children are allowed to suffer. It is forgotten that no child ever suffered anything yet except when some grown-up person has caused it to suffer by breaking the law of God.

Our country has a terrible record of cruelty to children, cruelty inflicted on children by their fathers and mothers, and though today physical cruelty is to some extent checked by law, and here we have no concentration camps, and no famine, we still have a form of cruelty, greater I think than all the others, certainly more lasting in effect, which is not even recognised as cruelty at all. Go and read the statistics of the divorce court, and see how many thousands of children have been betrayed by their mothers.

But how many of those who are shocked by the suffering of children would raise a finger to discourage divorce in England, with its continually rising tide of mental agony for children?

It is agreed by those who have been sufficiently devoted to make intensive observations that children have been much less affected by bombing than by evacuation. Loss of home, the sense of exile, often destroys a child's stability. Yet the evacuated children were not betrayed; they knew that they were sent away because their parents loved them. The children of divorced parents have no such consolation.

Delinquents, neurotics, criminals, addicts are nearly always the children of disunited parents, of wretched or lost homes, for they are people who see an imaginary enemy in all authority, and are always on the defensive. They are really defending themselves from the first authority that struck them a blow long ago.

Sadder still, these children meet every personal love that is offered them with hesitation, fear and sometimes even with hostility. They are afraid of being hurt by the only healing that there is. They build a hard shell around themselves and live in loneliness. Sometimes they seek escape in indulgence or vice. After all, we all want to escape from insecurity and loneliness, and there is no insecurity or loneliness to touch that of the child who in losing his mother has lost God.

'But he that shall scandalise one of these little ones that believe in me, it were better for him that a millstone should be hanged about his neck and that he should be drowned in the depth of the sea.'

What if it is the mother who scandalises? The best guarantee for the security of the child's home is his mother's goodness. 'Goodness' is a very unpopular word today. People, and young people in particular, have come to think of it as something drab and negative. They are afraid that if they are good they will miss something! The opposite is true: goodness means wholeness, completeness, integrity. It is the condition for being able to love uncompromisingly and completely, the condition for not missing reality.

Goodness is not got or kept without great supernatural activity. In this world it must be kept like a defended city.

Goodness is not got or kept without great supernatural activity. It means that all the supernatural faculties are intensely active and responsive and make one continually aware of God's love, just as a person whose natural senses are very acute is more aware of the beauty of a summer's day than, say, a person who is blind and deaf.

This awareness of God has to be worked for and kept, just as an artist has to work for and keep his vision of beauty. It is a mistake to suppose that the artist's insight and vision, or even his delight in what he sees, is inborn. It comes from long contemplation, from the ardours that go with acquiring skill, from concentration on his object, and above all from cutting out of his life everything that distracts or interferes. Thus he learns to select, to value by new standards, to treasure what has become for him the pearl of great price.

The acquiring and keeping of goodness is too hard a thing

to fallen nature without help from God. For every artist who achieves his vision, there are one hundred who relapse into a squalid frustration, because they have not will enough to meet the challenge made by their own spiritual hunger and thirst. They are one more example of 'Many are called but few are chosen'.

The help from God which makes goodness possible, and especially the help that mothers need for their special goodness, is the law of God.

'Law'—that is the second unpopular word that I have used! First 'goodness', then 'law'. People hate the idea of a law, of doing anything because they are commanded to do it. It is not the doing they mind but doing it because it is the will of God. They prefer their puny self-will to the ultimately irresistible law of love.

The examples of our Lady's attitude to the law, shown in the gospels of Christ's infancy, are to me the most outstanding thing we know of her, and once they were the most puzzling. How strange it seemed that the immaculate mother of God should submit herself to the ceremony of purification, for example. She did so and the world was to know it, they were to know that our Lady and St Joseph went to the temple with the infant Jesus and stood, unknown among a crowd of other peasants, holding the two white doves, the offering of the poor, in their hands. They fulfilled the law to the letter. It was so in everything. Read the gospel and you will find that our Lady and St Joseph kept the law with the carefulness with which people, when they are in love, carry out the requests of the beloved in the minutest detail.

That is the secret here, again the twofold love. Our Lady, knowing God as she did, knew that his law is the voice of love. It is not a litany of 'thou shalt not', but the vigilance of infinite love. Moreover, our Lady kept and loved the law not for herself alone, but for all the mothers of Christ yet to be, for all the unborn Christ-children who would need it for sword, and for shield, and for cloak.

The law is the hands of God cupped round the flame of life, tending it in the driving storm.

This goodness, this learning the law and keeping it should begin, not with the first child, but with the first doll. The child in the nursery learning her catechism in preparation for her first Communion is keeping faith with her own child, just as our Lady, as a tiny child, dancing for joy before the Holy of Holies, was keeping faith with the child Christ.

CANA

At the last supper, when our Lord was giving his body to the world in the blessed sacrament, his thoughts surely dwelt on the mother who had given him that body. It was on the evening before he died that the mystical body of Christ was being born into the unconscious world. Who could doubt that he was thinking of her, who was the mother of all the Christ-children to be in all the generations of men?

'A woman', he said, 'when she is in labour hath sorrow, because her hour is come; but when she has brought forth the child, she remembereth no more the anguish, for joy that a man is born into the world'. It is a mistake to think of our Lady's motherhood only in terms of suffering. Our little children who sing her seven sorrows, sing also her seven joys, and all her seven joys are one—the joy that Christ brought into the world.

Our Lord took all the world's sorrow to himself, but he did not bring it into the world. He brought no sorrow into the world, but he brought all its joy. For those who love God nothing is lasting except joy. All suffering, all sorrow, all parting, all pain, all death will pass; only joy will not pass.

The marriage at Cana is a showing of the joy that Christ brought into the world. Here, at his mother's request, our Lord worked his first public miracle. It is a delight to think that this first miracle was in no way connected with unhappiness. It was not healing sickness, forgiving sins or raising the dead; it was simply giving joy, more joy, to people who were already rejoicing.

It must have been a wonderful moment for our Lady, for she would have seen the changing of the water into wine as a symbol of the joy that her son would give, which would enter into men like wine, changing not the outward circumstances, but the inward being of everyone who received it, inebriating his heart and soul and mind with the love of God, as the senses are inebriated with wine. So that the world would be changed for him, would be different because he looked at it with different eyes, approached it with a different heart, looked at it with eyes lit up by vision, approached it with a heart warmed up by love.

God does not change, his laws do not change. He has given man free will, free will remains. The law of cause and effect remains. Man cannot use his free will against God and against God's law without building up an environment of suffering for himself. He has built a world for himself with stones of sorrow and now he must live in that world.

Our Lord did not bring this sorrow, but neither will he take it away, for if he took it away he would take away man's means to expiation. Instead Christ has wed himself to our sorrow, and by uniting it to himself he has changed it to joy. For the saints, sorrow and joy are one thing: love.

For those who are not saints and who do not know God, suffering has no meaning. In recent years we have piled up suffering for the human race to an extent which is frightening. Even the cynics, the indifferent and those who are frankly 'anti-God' know, with the instinctive realisation or fear, that somehow or other we must stay our hand of perish. It is a curious situation. Pride has lost faith in might; even the loveless are beginning to say out aloud that there is no hope but love.

It would not surprise me to wake up one morning and read in the daily press that a ministry of love had been set up, and on the next day it has broken up in chaos because nobody can remember what love is! To talk like this everyone replies with the air of someone voicing a startling, new and original idea: 'We need a change of heart.'

A change of heart is rather a vague term. We suppose, rather hopelessly, that it might mean that from being selfish, we become unselfish, from being suspicious, trusting, from being grasping, generous, and so on, and that this would happen without any effort from us, without any hard thinking, or risk, or bracing of the will. That we should just get up one morning to find a change of heart on the chair with our change of linen, and put it on hoping rather dubiously that it has not shrunk in the wash, as it was small enough before.

The change of heart, we think, would have to happen simultaneously to everyone, or it would be no good; in fact, if it happened to us and not to our enemies, it would even be a danger. But we console ourselves by a sneaking certainty that it could never really happen, because we know that for so long as fear remains in a heart, love can't get in, and we can't really see a logical reason for not being afraid.

But for all this it is true that a change of heart *is* the only thing that can begin to bring happiness back into the world. It is true too that it is not in our own power or strength to change our own hearts, and what is needed is a miracle.

First of all what must this change really be like? It must be an absolute change, a change like that which happens to a piece of grey cloth dipped into a crimson dye, and dyed all through. The symbol of the wine at Cana is apt: wine restores vigour to an exhausted man, warms him all through, brings colour back to his face, gives him courage, softens his heart, takes away his sense of insufficiency and sets him free.

The joy of God is a wine that changes the drab, cold, colourless substance of human nature into the rich, crimson, warm vitality of supernatural life. It changes discouragement to hope, doubt to faith, it lights up the mind and in its light men see that the problems of the world today, which seemed insurmountable, are straws in the power of God, and in his name even a creature as little and weak as man can overcome them.

How can such a change of heart happen? Only by a miracle it is true, and who can work such a miracle but Christ? When a man comes to this world with Christ in his heart, he too can work this miracle in Christ's name. This does not mean that every christian who carries Christ in his heart will be recognised as one who brings joy. No, the world will still hate him, in the proportion with which it hates Christ, Christ's purity, Christ's unworldliness, Christ's un-compromising truth. But in a few hearts that hatred will break down. To start with, the hate itself is born of fear. Poor human nature, that has lost the sweet intimacy with God that it once had, is afraid to accept the claim that Christ makes upon us, lest it would mean forfeiting what pleasure (the substitute for joy) we still have to console us for life and to distract us from death. Sometimes christians themselves are responsible for this tragic misunderstanding—those who divorce religion from the happy things in life and are kill-joys, puritans, the enemies of beauty.

In practice the miracle of Cana happening in the life of the christian works out very simply, and it is in this that the mother can so well help her child, by imitating our Lady. The fact that a man has supernatural life in his soul does not make him a genius, and he will indeed need all the wisdom that his mother learns from the mother of Christ.

It was his mother who brought Christ to the marriage feast, his mother who said to him 'They have no wine'. Now, too, the mother should encourage her son to go forward to the joyful occasions in life, to open his heart to the good things, to mix into its happiness, to enter into the hopes and delights and loves and dreams of other people, to be at the marriage feast. And it is she who can say to him 'Look! how little joy they have left after all, the wine of joy is running out. You who have Christ within can increase it for them, you can show them how to see the world through his eyes and so see its wonder, how to work with his hands and so restore the pleasure and dignity to their work, you can help them to listen to one another's voices with his ears and to love one another with his heart, and in this there is perfect joy'.

The mother knows, as our Lady did, that if Christ is *there* all will follow, if the seed of his life that she fostered in her child's heart is in flower in his manhood, that will be enough, the miracle will take place and where he goes there will be an increase of joy. She has learnt, through her life with her child, that joy begins within and radiates out, that the kingdom of heaven is within.

When Christ comes in a christian man to wherever God wants him to be, in that home or shop or office or workroom, the miracles can begin. The guests at Cana did not know the source of their good fortune. Often those who receive the wine of the joy of God are not aware that they have received it from one of their fellow workers or a close friend or even a relation. The miracle worker himself may not know it; it is enough for him to know that he is about his Father's business: the coming of Christ in an ordinary man to ordinary men, the quiet dispensation of the wine of his love everywhere. Love when it is joyful radiates, a few reflect its light, and the secret glory waxes into the world like morning into the sky. In some office or workroom or camp or home, a few unknown people begin to be faithful to an inviolate love—the world's healing has begun!

For the woman who, with Mary of Nazareth, loves with the twofold love, the love of God and the love of man, there can be no richer comfort than this one of seeing her son working the miracle of Cana. In this she will realise what it really means to have brought a man into the world, and from her own soul she can guess a little of the heaven in the heart of the girl who foresaw *her* joy as she sang her own on the hills: 'And his mercy is from generation to generation . . .'

And what of the deep contentment of our Lord himself, when on the evening before he died he changed not water into wine, but wine into blood, the blood that was to be the life stream of the man in all mankind. How tender a blessing he must have sent then to his mother, whose blood shone in his, in the ring of the little cup, and to all the mothers of all the Christs to be, all those mothers who would call upon his for help, and would go through travail upon travail of the heart and mind, that with her, they too might rejoice, forgetting all the sorrow that is past, for joy because a man is born into the world.

Our Lady

When I was a little girl, I was told by one in whom I had unlimited faith: 'Never do anything which you cannot imagine our Lady doing'. To this injunction was added the threat, 'If you do, she will blush'.

Such was the conception of our Lady imposed upon me by a pious upbringing, that I simply could not imagine her doing anything whatever that I did, and the attempt to do so frequently caused *me* to blush. It became an obsession, and since I could only imagine our Lady leaning on a cloud-bank or being a plaster statue, I finally sat still on a chair with closed eyes, until I broke down and sobbed with boredom and despair.

My conception of our Lady was a very common one, to many hundreds of Catholics she is unreal and even worse, unattractive. Most of our luscious (and frequently heretical) hymns are sung with complete insincerity. To many of us she is not lovable and we do not love her. No wonder, for nearly all we are taught of her by book and sermon is untrue, or probably untrue, the pious guess-work of not very clever sentimentalists.

Without any pretence, I can say that now, after about twenty years, I have learnt to love her and I do. What has caused the change? A stray remark from a realist started it. As I passed into a convent parlour to wait for a Reverend Mother, I heard a remarkable nun say to a girl: 'Stuff and nonsense—when our Lady was fifteen, she knew the facts of life from A to Z, the gospel proves it'.

That began my search, search for the real mother of God

in the gospel, for the facts about her. Another remark suddenly lit the facts I collected, made them come alive and flame up into a warm love. A young convert questioned about her answered: 'Our Lady?—oh well, I think of her as someone in whose skirts you can hide your face'.

The simple facts of the gospel which, after twenty years of thinking, are still not exhausted, indeed have only just been touched as it were with blind finger-tips are these:

> Our Lady gave God a human heart.
> She made it possible for him, for Christ, to love me.
> She gave her life to be his life.
> She gave him her body, what he asked for.
> She gave Christ his capacity for pain.
> Giving him life she gave him death.
> She was made for Christ and then literally her life became his life.
> She gave birth not only to the Christ in history, but to the Christ in all of us, she gave her good simple life to be the substance of his life in us.
> Her love for him always radiated, always went out to the whole world, always touched all sinners.
> When she held him to her heart, she took all broken sinful men to her heart.
> Giving him her life, she gave us our life.
> That is the great reality about her; she can truly say to him 'I am, that you shall have life, in every generation, and have it more abundantly. I am that you shall have life and have it in every christian heart'.

Simple facts, and only very few of them, found by reading the gospel to verify the splendid remark of the nun, overheard twenty years ago! And what secrets they contain, the secret of contemplation, of the mystical life, all the things we talk so glibly and foolishly of and yet long for so wistfully.

Nowadays there is a growing tendency to think of mysticism as a kind of Irish stew, made out of scrap-ends of

Buddha, Muhammed, Tolstoy and Einstein, to believe that if we can only manage to sit still with the sole of our foot flat on our stomach and respect fleas, we shall reach perfection.

No, it is a mistake, the sacramental life which is indeed the only true mysticism, the only pure contemplation, is the life that our Lady lived. It consisted in her daily self-giving of her life to make Christ's life, to give him birth, to give birth to him in all human beings. It was, and is, the life of sacramental love, the love which says and means: 'I want to give you the marrow of my bones, every cell of my body, the pulsing of my blood. It is not enough to be with you. to look at you, I must be in you, must be you. I want to be your food, your flesh and blood, yourself. I give you my body and I give it in every split second of every moment that I live, awake or asleep, in all that I do, in my words, in my work, in eating, laughing, weeping, in sorrow and in joy, that you may have my life and have it abundantly'. That is what our Lady's life said to our Lord Christ, that is what its tremendous littleness means. That is reality.

And she gave back to him the sort of love he had first given to her, for it is indeed her true son who says to all of us 'Take you all of this, this is my body, this is my blood'. That is our Lady, that is our Lord, that is reality, that is love.

Inscape

To the eye that sees, littleness reveals infinitely more than vastness. God is known more truly by a little finite creature through the contemplation of a snowdrop than through the contemplation of the universe. Very soon the intellect staggers before immensity, it is used up exhausted, only the rare heart responds to it at all. But the inward eye fills with light when it contemplates a little thing, the heart can fold upon it, and so the heart expands and the mind does not wither, but puts out petal upon lovely petal of thought.

Julian of Norwich cried out for joy when she took an acorn into her hand, not because she held an oak tree in a tiny casket, but because that smooth, oval, polished thing that fitted into the palm of her hand had life and its life was in it only through God, only because God its creator lived and gave it life!

From the universe we learn that God is infinite, that we cannot compass him at all. From such things as insects, flies, little frogs, mice and flowers we learn that to us he is something else. He is Father, brother, child and friend!

If you ever had a little green tree frog and watched him puffing out with a pomposity worthy of a dragon before croaking, you must have guessed that there is a tender smile on our heavenly Father's face, that he likes us to laugh and he laughs with us; the frog will teach your *heart* more than all the books of theology in the world.

It was fitting that Christ should choose a little and humble woman, hardly more than a child, to be his mother, to give him to us; to reveal his way with us. Mary knew that, knew

so well that her humility revealed his glory and the
immensity of his love more truly than any greatness could do.
She exalted in her littleness and then forgot it, because it led
her to the thought of him and that possessed her entirely.

He hath regarded the humility of his handmaid.
From henceforth all generations shall call me blessed;
He that is mighty has done great things in me.

She spoke like that in the ecstasy of the first advent, when his
life was a life hidden in her littleness, depending upon her for
its expression, when by his own will, his voice was silent
except for her words, his acts entrusted wholly to what she
did. She did many things and said very little. She paid the
loveliest and kindest visit recorded in history, her visit to
Elizabeth; she worked in her home, prepared her baby
clothes, looked after St Joseph. She suffered his doubt of her
silently, she obeyed the law and went to Bethlehem on the
eve of Christ's birth. In all that she did she showed Christ,
but perhaps most of all in her rejoicing in him, in her
rejoicing in the knowledge that his life would go on, not
bounded by time, for ever.

Telling her lovely secret to Elizabeth in the words of the
Magnificat, she already accepted the children of the world
whom Christ put into her arms when his own were spread
on the cross; more than that, her love swept out to them
across the centuries, giving him, giving her only child to
them. Just as she gave him his body to suffer cold and hunger
and thirst and death, and to rise from death, she gave him
to the children of men, to suffer over and over again in them,
to be cold and hungry and thirsty and to die over and over
again, and over and over again to rise from death. She knew
the cost to herself, but rejoiced: 'His mercy is from
generations to generations, to them that fear him'.

If we can learn of God from a snowdrop, how much more
can we learn of him from Mary's littleness! If the snowdrop
says to us 'In the white purity that comes out of the dark

earth God delights' does not Mary say to us 'In the life of thanksgiving, rejoicing, giving Christ, God's will is consummated'? Does not her self-forgetting say, 'forget yourself'? Her rejoicing in him say, 'rejoice in him'? Her Christ-giving say, 'give Christ'? To forget self, to delight in God, to give Christ—that is the eucharistic life, the only true thanksgiving for holy communion.

What is holy communion but Christ given to us, and we given to Christ, his words given to us to utter, his deeds to do, his beauty to reveal, his love to rejoice in, our littleness given to him? There are thousands of people with whom we come into contact who do not know Christ, who do not guess that he wants to be a brother, a lover, a child, a friend to them, who do not know that the gap, the emptiness they feel in their lives is there because God leaves it there on purpose, that they may hunger for his intimate presence, may accept the gift of himself! There is in every human heart, be it the heart of a man or a woman, an empty cradle, waiting for the birth of Christ to fill it. Those who have him, those in whom he is born again day after day, have just this one work to do, to show the others that what they want, what they long for, is Christ.

Let them see that 'the Lord is little and greatly to be loved' and they will do the rest. Books of theology can frighten them, noisy propaganda can drive them away, controversy can chill them, organisation withers up their minds, but the joy of someone like themselves, happy in the company of God, cannot fail to show them how lovable God is.

No one can fail to see when a friend has fallen in love and to guess, from the effects, with what sort of person they *are* in love. If that person is good, kind, reliable then the lover will come alive, they will sing at their work, they will have confidence, they will glow with a new warmth, a new tenderness. Everything round them will remind them of the person they love, so nothing will be dull or meaningless,

their very face will change. The plainest face is beautiful
when it is lit from within by love.

Their friends will think them lucky to be loved by this
person whom they have not met, but whose character is so
clearly shown by the new life, the radiant beauty of the one
who is loved; if their own life happens to be bleak, drab,
loveless, they will think wistfully how different *they* would be
if they too were loved like this!

The implication is obvious; the littleness of the individual
stressing the glory of God is his revelation to the world. No
one need be wistful for his love. 'Here', they can say, 'is
someone as weak and ordinary as I am, living my life, but
their communion with Christ has made them joyful and
vital and beautiful, it is an invitation to me to take him to
my heart too and live in his life'.

That is the eucharistic life—giving our littleness to God
and rejoicing in him, through our littleness giving him to the
world.

'Delight in the Lord and he will give you the desires of
your heart'.

Our Mother and I

The thought which stands out in my mind as an incentive to pray for the missions is that there is not one person created for whom Christ would not have suffered and died, if that one was the only one to be saved. Each one human being is all to God. The whole of his infinite love is given to each. In this light what a tragedy it is that there can be people who have never heard the name of Christ, and how logical that those who love him find it worth the sacrifice of self to make him known and loved to people, such for example as the Aborigines, who to those who do not know or love God and who live far off in over-civilised cities seem hardly other than a particular kind of plant that grows in a partly explored country!

The missionary takes more than the knowledge of Christ. He or she takes Christ himself. Priests take Christ in the sacraments. But women take Christ too. To make this clear I will tell you what a priest said to me once, years ago. He had been in a persecuting country and imprisoned. He escaped, but with both his hands cut off. He said 'Never again can I lift up Christ in my hands, but I can lift him up in my heart and so can you. You can take Christ everywhere, show him to everyone. Be his monstrance'.

The first woman who was Christ's monstrance, who had a missionary heart, was our Lady. This is why it is natural to pray to her for the missions and for missionaries. When we do so we are not even asking a favour of her, but are only asking her to do what is clearly her own desire.

She was, and of course is, compelled by a twofold love,

which is the key to her human personality, two loves so inseparable, that in her they are one love. The love of God and the love of man.

Her own glorious expression of this love in words is the *Magnificat* in which our Lady, rejoicing in the wonder of her motherhood, rejoices most of all, not in her personal delight, but in the fact that her son will go on his quest of the human heart from generation to generation. We find it difficult to make people in other lands real to us in spite of all the knowledge we can have of them from those who have lived with them, in spite of all the modern invention which makes distance an unreality. But to that girl, for she was just a girl, living in a tiny hamlet two thousand years ago, with only her own heart to inform her, all people in all generations were vividly real. Her imagination went out to them, sweeping through time like a flame, a flame of the fire of living love, incarnate in her. The first petition, therefore, that I make to our Lady is that I may learn through the love of God to know all men, that my imagination may be made large with love.

Our Lady is a practical inspiration to missionaries, one to whom we may surely entrust them in all their journeys. Her first instinct, even before she saw Christ's face, while he was still hidden in her womb, was to take him to others who needed him, to take him to them to give them life. In the wonderful story of her visit to Saint Elizabeth, we find the first perfect missionary journey.

There is another striking way in which our Lady is very close to those who love God and man, and who are seeking to know their own personal vocation, perhaps whether to be a missionary or not, and if so how and where. Our Lady solved that by her complete surrender to God to do his will. Her prayer at the annunciation is the perfect prayer for any and everyone sincerely seeking light to know and the will to do what God asks of him. 'Let it be unto me according to thy word'. That prayer accepted everything that could lead to God's will, and so will it for us. First of all to that great will of love that he has for us all, that Christ be formed in us. Then to our taking Christ in us wherever he wants to go to, being where he wants us to be, being what he wants us to be.

In our Lady's case it certainly led to a real missionary life. Her second missionary journey was through the desert into Egypt and to years of exile in a strange land, and her last was to Calvary and the tomb of Christ. She will certainly show, to all who ask her, the way for them to follow. She has already told us how to be sure of the way in the one command she is recorded to have spoken, 'Do whatever he tells you' (Jn 2:6).

From anyone else this command, uncompromising and austere as it is, might be frightening. To us, weak creatures, the idea of a complete, final surrender often is frightening, but that is because we do not know God well enough. The fact is that God's will for us is always for our happiness and when we do surrender to it, it is to our own happiness that we are abandoning ourselves.

We can trust our Lady's love for us too and her knowledge of God. The woman who says 'Do whatever he tells you', is the girl who sang the *Magnificat*, rejoicing that her son had come for our joy, and this first miracle, symbol as it is of Christ's life in us, was not a miracle related to suffering, but one designed to give an increase of joy to people already rejoicing. That good wine is a symbol of Christ's life in our soul, changing our tepid, colourless human nature to the strong life-giving humanity of Christ, and giving it the power to invigorate others, to warm their hearts and minds, to kindle the life in them with Christ's love, just as wine given to a cold weary person tones up the blood in their veins.

So it is logical to pray to our Lady, first for the missionaries, that they may carry Christ to those whom he loves as she carried him to Saint Elizabeth, so that he may give life to those to whom he is taken as he did by his presence in Mary to the unborn John the Baptist, second for ourselves, that we may be dyed through and through with

the colour and taste and power of Christ, through having
given ourselves over wholly and unreservedly to God's will.
Pray that in our apostolate, which is our own mission too,
wherever we are we may not have the depressing effect of
cold water on other people, but the bright, glowing effect of
strong wine, the quality of joy that our mother knows to be
the inevitable result of her own prayer on our lips, 'Let it be
done unto me according to thy word'.

Mothers of the Unseen Christ

The instinct for motherhood should be predominant in women, result of the capacity for love. There are not many in whom the capacity for love is dead or so withered up that it is nearly dead. But if it is questionable whether this instinct can die, it can turn inwards and destroy where it should create, it can produce hardness where it should produce tenderness. This is not negative, it is a tremendous force wrongly used.

Nature, and by that is meant human nature with its full capacity for love, is the means of holiness. God made and used very simple things for his sacraments and through his sacraments he gives us his life in this world. He chose wine and bread for the supreme sacrament and sacrifice, the sacramentals are water and oil and salt. Our life too is sacramental, but for the sacramentals of our life he chooses equally simple things, our instincts, our emotions, our desires, all the things which make us human beings.

For some marriage is a vocation; it is a superb vocation, on it depends not merely our race going on, but the Christ-life going on in the world. But there are others who have the vocation to be spiritual mothers. Sometimes they are married women too and learn this spiritual motherhood from their own children, but sometimes they are unmarried, either from choice or circumstance. I say 'circumstance' because it is a cruel mistake to suppose that if a woman would honestly like to marry but circumstances make it impossible, that she is merely frustrated and should devote her life to toy dogs, bazaars and acidity.

Circumstance is the *one* reliable test of God's will for us, and a clearer indication of vocation than any 'attraction' we may feel.

For the woman, then, who does not marry, is motherhood a vocation? It most certainly is, and God forbid that anyone shall read into those words the condoning of that fussy, grasping interfering attitude that passes so often for 'spiritual motherhood'. The first essential thing is this, that the mother instinct, the capacity for love, be awake, alive.

This means suffering. It is easier in the long run to dry up the life in us than to develop and direct it. The woman who will be truly a spiritual mother will feel in herself, in her body and in her soul all the desire and the necessity for a child of her own.

In this very passionate longing, in this aliveness of love her purity will consist. Indeed it is the essence of virginity, for we do not lay dead ash on the altar of sacrifice but burning fire. This same intense aliveness gives her a constant suffering. All maternity involves pain and sacrifice, spiritual maternity as much as any other.

Then again she has to think this, that it is for the sake of the spiritually motherless children that God asks her to suffer this lifelong depth of feeling, which so far as her personal gratification is concerned will always be unsatisfied. He wants her to be hungry and thirsty all her life. This is achieved only by the development of her nature and complete abandonment to his will.

For whom is this hunger and thirst? For whom does God ask women to develop their human nature to its full warmth and tenderness and to sacrifice it? For the child Christ.

The child Christ lives in many souls, disregarded, unfostered, unhelped. It is not only in the sinner that he needs a mother, but in timid and ignorant souls, in souls where his innocent life is suffocated by worldliness, in souls surrounded by subtle temptations to so compromise with faith and holiness that were there no mother to help and counsel and make strong, his life could never come to be more than a sickly colourless flower growing in a dark cellar.

Suffering and Love

Advent

LIGHT

The thought of God is the thought of light. 'Let there be light' are the first words of creation, God's will for the world.

He dwells in 'light inaccessible' (1 Tim 6:16) and with him since before the beginning of time, before the sun and the moon and the stars were made, his eternal Word, Jesus Christ, who is the light of the world: the Morning Star, the light shining in darkness, who was promised to us in the sign of a woman standing on the moon, whose birth shone in a star.

> In him there was life, and that life was the light of men; and the light shines in the darkness, darkness was not able to master it (Jn 1:4).

Advent is an urgent longing for the dawn of Christ's light in the world. Its lovely liturgy gathers up the desire of the suffering people of God waiting in the darkness for the incarnation, and carries it on a great wave of hope, down the centuries into our time. It concentrates the longing of the whole world in each heart that longs for Christ's coming, and puts upon each tongue the age-old prayer that well might have been written today for us:

> Dawn of the East, brightness of the Light Eternal, and Sun of Justice, come and enlighten them that sit in the darkness and in the shadow of death (Greater antiphons 21 December; cf Ps 107:14).

God is light, Christ is the shining out of the light of God. The property of light is to illuminate, to give beauty to all it touches, to heal all that it penetrates, to purify all that is submitted to its heat. The incarnation is the dawn of Christ's light in us. Our longing for that dawn is our prayer for the world, our surrender of self to him, is our gift of Christ to men.

There is a widespread idea today that it does not matter what our conception of God is like; how vague it is, how confused, even how distorted. 'We all worship the same God' has become almost a shrug of the shoulders, dismissing the responsibility of knowing God as he reveals himself to be, as if to know him truly made no difference to us.

But as our conception of God is, so we ourselves become. If we think he is hard, we grow hard; if we think he is a kill-joy we become kill-joys, if we think of him as an omnipotent secret police, all-present, all-seeing, all-terrible, we shrink from him, and the heart that shrinks from God shrinks to nothing.

Saddest of all misconceptions is the merely negative God; it is this that fills the world with negative, apathetic people, futile before the misery of mankind. Only Christ's light can touch that misery. Only in that light shining within us can we see the long-obscured path back to human happiness and walk in it.

Certain moralists delight in depicting the path to happiness, which incidentally is the path to heaven, as not only straight and narrow but dark treacherous and impassable, with the result that human initiative dries up, and courage is sapped at the outset.

Hard it is and beset with danger, but we are not asked to walk in it blindly; with Christ in our heart we see every step of the way. Light, St Paul tells us, is armour, the feet set in Christ's crimson footprints are shod in flame.

It is the particular tragedy of today that so many people have lost their faith in mammon and have not found it in

God, because of the wrong conception of him that is printed upon their imagination. There is nothing to attract them to seek for him.

Religion, they say, is an escape, but it is the only escape that they do not try. For a man who has slammed the door on God must try to escape from the emptiness in the house of his soul. The solitude that is sweet is to be alone with God; to be shut up alone with oneself is more than human nature can bear.

Man has a good appetite for beauty and for pleasure, but he does not perceive the measure of good that is in them if his mind is not illuminated with the ray of the divine light. If it were he would know that even his highest pleasures, the delights of the mind, are only shadows of eternal joy, more distinct when they are thrown sharp and clear on a page that reflects such brilliance.

And in every passing, simple happiness, in the brief loveliness of the senses, the multitudinous beauty of the world, though it be swift as a shooting star or a wing in flight, he would know the eternal now.

His escapes fail him, or perhaps it is truer to say he fails them. In the end he withers away from his pleasures like a brown leaf that falls from the tree and is trodden into the earth. Had he seen in Christ's light, he would have known that even in the escapes from self that this world can offer there is no escape from the invitation of the overflowing love that is God, and death is but a passage through the dreams of darkness to the reality of dawn.

It would be useless if not odious to preach to the Christ-blind people of the world. What the world needs is to see. Even a blind man can see a bright light through his darkness. We can give the light of God to the world by giving our hearts to the light of God.

Christ's way is unchanging, he comes into the world through individual lives. In the individual heart is the world's redemption. He comes to those who desire him, to the heart that is given to him to shelter his light, and to each he comes as he came to Mary, for the whole world. He is not confined by our limitations or hidden by our darkness, his light irradiates from our heart and illuminates the world, he is always the light that shines in darkness.

The conception of God as light, reiterated all through the liturgy and echoing in particular loveliness through the Advent prayers, draws the mind to long for Christ's coming too, with the longing of darkness for daybreak or the tender shoot in the earth for the heat of the sun.

In that longing and in its increase is the world's hope. The church answers it in Christ's name:

> The Lord will come and will not tarry, and will bring to light the hidden things of darkness and will manifest himself to all nations (Vespers, 3rd Sunday in Advent).

GROWTH

The patience of the countryman is visible on his face. He sets his pace to the pace of nature, to the great rhythm of the seasons. He measures in cycles of darkness and of light. He does not complain because the time in which summer's glory slumbers is so long in proportion to its flower and fruit. He is always conscious of the presence of the life whose beauty he sees so briefly.

He does not grudge that life his service, the monotony of its unvarying, exacting routine, the early rising, the manual labour, the ceaseless watching, the wrestle with the forces that seem stronger than man. Storm, drought, frost, blight, choking weeds. Stronger than man they may be, but he knows that they are not stronger than the life in all living.

Neither is he, who knows the earth, impatient of the winter. When day is short and dark, when night comes early and nature sleeps, he is content to sit by the fire in the long silent evenings and slumber too.

He accepts the law of growth and lives by it. Like life in the earth Christ grows in us. He is, St Paul says, formed in us. The supernatural growing is a slow ordered process of which natural life is a shadow.

Before Christ flowers visibly in our lives, he must, as he has ordained, fulfil his own law of growth in us. It was his will to grow in Mary, to grow in his humanity, from babyhood to boyhood, from boyhood to manhood, to grow not only in body but in wisdom and grace.

Now it is his will to grow in us, gradually, gently, assimilating our lives to himself. There will be seasons in which we feel no stir of the life within us, see nothing but the earth's hard crust. Then the daily conquest of sin will be as exacting as the daily pulling up of weeds that grow as fast as they are pulled.

Every honest Catholic knows how useless it sometimes feels to go on day after day finding the same sins cropping up in the examination of conscience, week after week confessing the same sins, the same number of times! He *feels* it is useless, but *knows* that he does it so that when at last the supernatural life pierces the hard ground, it will not be choked.

We shall sometimes be surrounded by forces that threaten the inward life, forces stronger than we are ourselves. But though only faith can convince us of this, they are not so strong as the unheard, unseen, unfelt, unimaginably sensitive Christ-life within us, that is stronger than the storming, parching, freezing or blighting of any possible environment.

We must not abandon the struggle that the secret growing demands, or doubt its purpose: the getting up early on dark mornings for mass when our presence at mass has become only a losing fight with distractions, the offering of our daily work to form Christ in us when the monotony of our daily work makes it seem incapable of any meaning at all.

But neither must we refuse the slumber, the repose, of the winter time of growth, the stillness, the silence, the acceptance of the times set by God, God's law of growth, the contented folding of our life upon the hidden life within us. It is in these mysterious winters of the Spirit that we must learn patience with ourselves. Not complacency, but the humility based on self-knowledge, which is not surprised if there is little if any outward change, because what change there is, is in the inward increase of Christ, and that God sees, but men do not.

Sometimes pride is amazed that there is no show of virtue for our pains; a vulgarity of vanity demands the forced, showy bloom of hot-house virtues, instead of being content to wait for the natural, ordered flowering of Christ's humility. Or we become anxious, like children who dig up the seed to see if it is growing, and alas we tend not only to scratch and dig in our own patch of dirt but in our neighbour's too. We are astonished at our failings, scandalised at his, particularly in his conduct to us.

Sometimes criticism of our neighbour, our imposition on him of our own standard or ideal, which may not be God's standard and ideal for him, starts him turning and sifting and worrying his own poor little plot of dust; disturbing, perhaps destroying the first delicate thrust of supernatural life growing quietly in it.

We forget that Christ chooses to become man, not to become angel, not to descend from the clouds, blazing in his glory to live among us—but to grow hidden in heavy clay, out of sight, assimilating our humanity to his, willing to pierce our clay with the little green spear of his love at the appointed hour, to break forth, not from the stars, but from the humanity that is dust and dirt.

How much more often we would behold the glory of the Word made flesh if during this time of growing we forebore to comment on one another's peculiarities and shortcomings, and instead treated one another with the courtesy that we would have shown our Lady, had we been with her during the months before Christ's birth. It is to her that we must

turn in Advent, to learn the lessons of acceptance and
gentleness. Acceptance of God's mysterious ways with us, of
his timing and his law, and the lesson of gentleness, the
bringing courtesy to Christ, small and secret and silent in one
another's hearts.

Then we, at last apprehending dimly the wonder and joy
of the miracle of love repeated from generation to generation
in the eternal mystery of the incarnation, may pray with the
prophet Isaiah, for ourselves, for our fellow christians and for
the whole world

> Let the earth be opened and
> bud forth a Saviour.

JUSTICE AND LOVE

It is a disconcerting fact that while the Lord who comes to
us in holy communion is exactly the same person who will
come to us on the day of judgement, we long for his coming
in the one case and dread it in the other. We feel that we
know him instinctively now, but then he will be a stranger,
that Christ the lover and Christ the judge are two different
people. Of course they are not, they are one and the same,
and in God justice and love are one and the same thing.

So far our Lord's approach to us on earth has been
amazingly tender. He has come as a child, as bread, as an
inward presence like light. But how different will his last
coming be! It is this coming, as much as the incarnation, and
his birth in our soul, that the church sets before us in Advent
and bids us face.

Listen to Christ telling of it. The conditions we know too
well today, wars, famines, ideology, betrayal of one another's
blood, withall false teachers rising up on every side to
confuse a broken-hearted world. All this will be but 'the
beginning of travail' to increase human anguish, until Christ

tells us 'There would have been no hope left for any human creature, if the Lord did not cut these days short' (Mk 13:20).

Then suddenly, unexpectedly, Christ will appear, a king of glory. The sun fired from a spark of his light will blaze and burn out, the stars will fall out of rocking skies. The wings of legions of angels will sweep the world, driving the whole human race to the judgement throne of God. And now, as if he were changing the subject, though he is not, our Lord says an indescribably warm and tender thing.

> Now of the fig tree learn a parable, when the branch thereof is now tender, and the leaves are come forth, you know that summer is very near (Mk 13:28).

How moving that is, in the midst of the power and the glory, the little silky leaf uncurling its delicate pale green, reaching out a tiny hand for the promised splendour. But it is not just the poetry that goes home, but the implication that the day of judgement will after all be a summer! Not destruction, but fulfilment; not a withering, but fruition!

It will be the birth for which humanity has been in travail. The suffering, the labour, the patience, that what was hidden will bear fruit, the fruit will be red on the bough. The ugliness that disfigured grief will give place to beauty. The blood spilt in the dust will blossom like a rose.

'The summer is very near'. The summer! That is what justice is. The mind sweeps back to Christ's first coming, when the heart that will rock heaven beat in the tiny pulse of a peasant girl, and she cried out joyfully: 'He has put down the mighty from their seat and exalted the Lowly!' Justice is the winter of arrogance, the summer of lowliness.

When the angels gather the risen dead from their graves, from the depths of the sea, from the furnace, from under the ruins of their cities, the torn, the twisted, the mutilated, the broken dead, the young, the beloved dead, the remembered and the forgotten dead, they will come together, whole and beautiful, radiant in the joy of their now visible Christ life.

Before we lift our eyes to the glory of the King's face, we shall see it mirrored on theirs; their eyes will first look upon us with the eyes of the Judge. If we knew them before, and some of them we certainly did, we knew them with the dirt, the blood, the spittle of the world on their faces. The question will grip our hearts, holding them, waiting for the answer, in which is heaven or hell for us. Was it we who wiped away the tears and blood and revealed Christ's face? If not, it can only have been our fault. We lived in a century that tried to hustle suffering away behind the walls of institutions, but was not able to hide Christ or his passion or his need.

The walls were broken down, the Son of Man had nowhere to lay his head, he was stripped naked before our eyes, scourged, mocked, dragged from one civil servant to another, unjustly tried, condemned and crucified. His hands and feet were continually being hammered on the cross, drowning the humming of our machines, with the ringing of iron hammer on iron nail.

We of this generation will hardly be able to ask on the day of judgement: 'Lord, when was it that we saw thee hungry, or thirsty, or a stranger, or sick, or in prison——?' If for some reason we cannot take an active part in the works of love the world cries out for, we *can* recognise Christ in every man in every nation. We can close our minds against prejudice, we can live in communion with the whole world. We can pray in Christ's power.

If we have nothing material to give, we have poverty, if not bodily strength, we have weakness, if we have nothing else, we have ourselves. When Christ gave himself, in the manger, on the cross, he was poor, naked, weak. He had only himself. And what we have we can share with the nearest at hand, can divide with those who are in need with us.

The risen Christ was known in the breaking of bread. May

he know us on the morning of our resurrection, through the breaking of our bread with humanity today. Today each of us will pass sentence on his own heart. Today we will choose either the terror of the *Dies Irae* or the summer that is very near.

PEACE AND COURAGE

Longing for peace is the one bond between the people of the world. Like the seed, unseen, striving towards the light, it may suddenly flower simultaneously everywhere. Its flowering may show that despite the differences that antagonise, the things that we hold in common are the loveliest things: the tender love of God, true human values.

Peace is Christ's culminating gift. At his birth the angels' song mingled with the first bleating of the Lamb of God, promising peace to God's friends. On the night before he died his own promise comforted his apostles; when he had risen from the dead his first words to them were 'Peace be upon you'.

How is it then that peace is so rare, even in our soul? It may be because we lack the courage without which true peace is unattainable, and with or without which the pseudo-peace we have built up in our imagination is unattainable. That is a passive state in which nothing will ever disturb or threaten, which no temptation will assail, which depends on good health, a good bank balance, good esteem, and by the miracle that could push a camel through the eye of a needle, an untroubled conscience.

It is an immense relief to know that Christ's peace is not in the least like that which the world gives, or in weak moments imagines. 'I do not give peace as the world gives it', and then, both tenderness and warning, 'Do not let your heart be disturbed or play the coward'.

The condition of peace is courage, but the moments in

which we most long for it are those when courage seems most
difficult. When all that we want is to loosen our hold, to
throw off responsibility, to rest. We want not a sword, but
a lap big enough to bury our head on.

It is comfort then to realise that the courage peace
demands is in fact to relax, to throw all our care into the lap
of God. It means that we must take the risk of trusting God's
love, believing Christ's word, loving one another.

When Christ wept over Jerusalem, a Jerusalem that is
surely London, New York, and Moscow too, he said: 'Ah, if
thou couldst understand, above all in this day that is granted
to thee, the ways that can bring thee peace'. He has told us
these ways in the Sermon on the Mount. We must know God,
the Father whose delight is not only to give each one all he
needs, but to give it clothed in beauty, life in shining water,
bread in a million grains of gold. To know all men as God's
children, therefore our brothers, to be pure because we live
in God's light, carefree because we trust in his love. To
become children in heart, that here and now we may possess
the kingdom of heaven.

A child knows no anxiety, if he knows himself to be loved,
no mistrust or suspicion. His values are true. He loves things,
but he loves them not for what they cost, but for what they
are. To the chagrin of worldly aunts, he prefers the old blind
Teddy Bear to the most expensive new toy. Surely God
smiled at the poet in the child when he hid the rare diamond
in the rock and scattered large handfuls of frosted glass upon
the sea shore. Poverty may come, the child knows his father
will provide his happiness; pain may come, his mother's hand
will take it away. He is not worldly because he lives in a
secret world of his own. No one can take his kingdom from
him because it is not of this world.

Our peace too is in the spirit of childhood, in the secret
kingdom, the kingdom of heaven within us, where the Christ
child is king. It does not mean that we shall no longer fight.
Temptation will still be temptation, suffering will still be

suffering, the world will still be the world, menacing, ruled by the prince of darkness. But the world will not destroy us.

The peace of Christ is Christ. There is no other. 'I have said this to you that in me you may find peace. In the world you will only find tribulation, but take courage. I have overcome the world'. How often in Christ we see peace and tribulation together. At his birth, the angels' song of peace echoes among the cries of the first little martyred innocents. On Maundy Thursday his peace and his passion draw close to one another. The risen Christ shows his wounds and bestows his peace in one gesture of love.

All this extends to world peace. We cannot have Christ's peace without Christ. We cannot have Christ without his whole uncompromising Truth, without his Passion, his defence of the small and weak, his justice and his all-including love. The kiss of peace, given at the altar, cannot be replaced, however diplomatically, by the kiss of Judas given at the conference table.

At the mass the story of Christ's gift of peace is shown again. It is after the consecration, when in a mysterious manner Christ is born, and before the communion that we pray urgently for peace, and we pray to the Lamb of God: 'Lamb of God who takest away the sins of the world grant us peace'. The lamb is symbol of innocence and infancy and sacrifice. We ask him for peace, and immediately in communion he gives us himself.

So is it that peace on earth can be restored through the hearts of the unknown, humble people in all the countries of the world who open their hearts to the Lamb of God that in them the whole world's peace may begin.

Advent is closing and the longing of the church for light and for the spring, the budding forth of the saviour, is culminating in the mystery of Christmas, and we can put aside our cares to make the house of our soul ready for the child, with prayer as simple as a folk song, rocking the cradle of peace to the beating of the human heart.

Lent and Easter

THE WILDERNESS

In the wilderness Christ experienced the temptation that faces everyone today. The temptation to the ideals of materialism, presumption and power.

'Bid these stones turn into loaves of bread'.

It is all too easy for us, shocked by the world's hunger, to think that 'bread only'—material good—is happiness. Easier because we know that if we do not feed the hungry we will surely hear Christ's voice saying—'I was hungry and you did not give me to eat'.

Millions too, worn down by hour after hour in food queues, week after week of bitterly taxed wages, year after year trying to stretch the same monotonous minimum to feed the same difficult man, growing children and fastidious invalids, feel no heart left to hunger for more than material bread. Yet 'Man can not live by bread only, there is life for him in all the words that proceed from the mouth of God'.

All created things are words of God, light, darkness, water, fire, the smallness of children, the friendship of animals, science, rhythm, poetry, music, art, the tenderness of mothers, the ardours of lovers. Above our heads, under our feet, within our hearts, words of God whisper and laugh and sing one thing: 'See how I love you!'

It is good to work for material bread, to be grateful for it, but bad to be satisfied by it, terrible to be sated by it—not to hunger for the love that gives life, to be content to live without wonder, impotent in the eternal arms.

When Christ looked out over 'all the kingdoms of the world', he saw our cities today, London, Paris, Berlin, Moscow, New York, in all their splendour and all their squalor, their cinemas and restaurants, their churches and brothels, their luxury flats and their slums, their parks and their docks. He saw the shambles of our bombed cities, he saw Nagasaki and Hiroshima—'The kingdoms of the world and the glory of them!'

Just think, that young man consumed by a passion of love for humanity, suddenly the whole world spread out under his eyes, and its destiny put into his hands if he will take it on Satan's terms, absolute power to replan, rebuild, to impose his will upon the world. When he had refused, what had he left to bring to the world's suffering, to give his message of joy?

His limitations were straighter than those of any modern disciple. Poor, unknown, without influential friends, no press, no radio, no speed, no travelling, only one language. Miracles? Then as now they convinced no one who did not want to believe; then 'worked by Satan', now 'a natural explanation or a fake'.

Christ had only himself, his body, his human soul, his voice, his prayer, his heart. Three short years to live, his words already numbered, his footsteps counted, in his time his message would carry as far as the wind carried his words, as far as his footprints marked the dust.

What have *we* to bring to the hunger and sorrow of the world? We have ourselves, but what selves! Empty husks, threadbare as our clothes, our five senses starved by austerity. How can supernatural life be quickened in us, let alone through us in the world?

Christ had only himself, we have much more, ourselves and Christ in us. 'You have only to live on in me' he says 'and I will live on in you', and again 'It is I who am the bread of life'. It is he who is the ultimate word of God, the Word, telling the whole secret of the love that is our life.

We are not asked to see beyond the visible world with our
eyes, but with Christ's vision, and he is light. We must see
with Christ's eyes, hear with Christ's ears, heal with Christ's
hands, speak with Christ's words, live with Christ's life.
Above all we must love with Christ's heart.

Only love can give life.

Only Christ's love can redeem and forgive and illumine.
Only Christ's love can waken the world from apathy to
wonder.

Only Christ's love can quicken the world with new life.
Love is given only in man's gift of himself. There is no
other way.

Christ had only himself. He has given himself to us, that
we may love the world with his love and that the world
may live.

THE BREAKING OF BREAD

When we have something to suffer, big or small, it fills our
consciousness, seeming unbearable until we compare it with
the world's suffering, then it dwindles to a fragment. But
there is no comfort in knowing that others suffer more, and
the more we realise the world's suffering, the more do we
long to help it and the more helpless we feel to do so.

Yet it is a fact that our fragment can relieve the sorrow of
all mankind. Because Christ is in us any suffering of ours is
his passion. He took all human suffering, great and small,
and wed himself to it, crowned it with his crown of thorns,
clothed it in his purple garment, gave it the power of his
love. Christ's passion redeems, not because it is our pain, but
because it is his love infused into our pain.

We are all responsible for the world's suffering because we
are all sinners; sin becomes one great load of suffering on the
back of mankind. Men, women and children, even animals
'groan together with him'. Each time we commit what we

dare to call a 'little' sin we reach out our hand to put one more weight on the scale of human misery. Each sin becomes all suffering.

We all share the responsibility for suffering, equally we are all trustees of Christ's love. More, we own his passion, it is ours to spend, or to waste by resisting the power which makes our fragment of sorrow potent to redeem. Each one owes mankind his personal suffering. The power of our suffering is not measured by its magnitude but by our will to give.

One good thing has resulted from the war, our awareness of our dependence on one another. We know now that without wholeness, humanity at one with itself, there will be no happiness. Everyone is talking about unity. They have realised at last that it cannot be achieved by force or persuasion, by everyone wearing the same black shirt or red tie, or even the same bright smile! Oneness is organic, it doesn't give all men the same hat, the same temperament or even the same worldly chance, it does give them the same life. It is closer than brotherhood, closer than marriage, closer than a mother to her unborn child. It is the oneness of man with himself. It is the blood stream of humanity, one life in all living, one man in all men, the only real oneness possible, Christ in us.

The breaking of bread at mass symbolises Christ's suffering. In each fragment of the broken host, Christ is whole, in each fragment of human suffering his passion is whole. By a wonderful provision of pity, each fragment of sorrow is the whole of the world's suffering and the suffering of the whole world can never be more than one man can suffer. In holy communion, millions of small hosts are given to millions of people; this does not mean that Christ is divided into millions, but that the millions are made one in Christ.

A flesh and blood example tells more than many words. I was at mass in a side chapel where I knew the priest would have no communion hosts. But at the *Domine non sum dignus* a woman came out of the shadows and whispered 'Come, he has one host for me, he will divide it'. I turned and saw poverty, suffering that shamed me, a woman in rags, her face burnt and hardly human, only the eyes that looked out of it shone with unbelievable serenity. The priest divided the host reserved for her between us. She gave Christ to me, Christ's passion to the world.

At first sight suffering seems broken up, unfairly divided. In reality it is the human race that is divided, suffering is a communion which makes us one, as sacramental communion does. We can give Christ's passion to one another, as the poor woman gave Christ to me, and we can comfort Christ in one another in doing so.

A child, mortifying his thirst on a hot day, can moisten the lips of Christ in an army camped in the desert. A martyr dying from exposure in frozen Siberia can give Christ's death to a student shivering in London because he has no shilling for his gas.

May the breaking of the bread of our sorrow make us one in the passion of Christ. At the last supper Christ took bread into his hands and broke it: 'Then he took bread and blessed and broke it and gave it to them saying, this is my body.' In the old law, the breaking of the bread at the feast of Passover was a commemoration of the suffering of the Jews in captivity. Christ used this gesture of sorrow to give us his body on the night before he died; he gave us his passion in his body, gave us himself, his suffering and his sacrifice, his heart full of compassion and his hands so soon to be nailed for all time to the hard wood of our suffering.

In his hands we can offer our fragment for the world, just as the priest offers the host at mass. In this sense we are all priests, because we are all 'Other Christs'. It is estimated that there are four elevations every second in every twenty-four hours. We see the host lifted in the priest's hands at our local altar. Who can estimate how many elevations God sees from the altars of man's heart, in factories, kitchens, schools, workhouses, hospitals, ships and camps all over the world.

THIS IS MY BODY

The most universal suffering in England today is the sense of personal futility: faced with the huge burden of the world's suffering we feel helpless to help at all. This sense of futility is brought home to us whenever we come face to face even with one person's grief. What for example can we say or do, when a friend is bereaved of his child? Nothing at all, it seems.

This feeling has become aggravated by the fact that the need to 'Do something' has become almost a disease. Very often too it is only an escape from realising our own futility, or worse, an escape from *being* something. Many little groups that do things, though not necessarily the right things, become pigmy worlds, in which the universe is lost sight of and the doing is valued not by its effect on the whole world, but by the accumulation of fuss that can be crowded into one day's activity. But mercifully many people have no opportunity even for such escapes, and become hopelessly discouraged by their limitation of circumstances, ability, energy, opportunity, environment, so that the suffering which used to be particularly that of old or invalid people is spreading among everyone like a disease. 'What', they ask, 'have I got?': 'What can I do?'

Everyone has a body. Everyone can make the prayer of the body. It is a total act of love for the world. It is a searching contemplation of Christ.

It is possible for everyone, always, if they have a body. It means offering our bodies as a sacrifice for mankind. It needs no sweet meditation, no eloquence of words, no sensible fervour. It can be made in aridity, weariness, dullness, boredom, pain, in temptation, in any circumstances at all, by anyone.

It can be made by schoolchildren sitting still in class, by workers getting up on cold dark mornings, by office workers disciplining their bodies to the routine of bus, train, the office chair, the office tea, the rush hour, by lovers using the restraint of selfless tenderness, by people in the grip of pain, by sick people, and by old people in the humility of just being very weak, very sleepy and very old.

The worst of all mistakes, one often made by pious people, is to separate soul and body, the worst snobbery that which despises the body. For practical purposes soul and body are one. The prayer of the body is the sacrifice of self.

Christ's prayer of the body began at the annunciation. It has not ended, it goes on in the host, the risen body, and in us. It was offered in the first shiver in Bethlehem, in the stretch and ripple of his muscles in Nazareth, in his hunger in the wilderness, in his thirst in Samaria, his tears over Jerusalem, his sweat in Gethsemane, in his blood on the cross, in his rising from death, in his working, eating, sleeping, hearing, seeing, speaking, touching and breathing.

There are very many lives that are one with the life of Christ's body in the host. Think of that life, silent, restricted, small, helpless, dependent on his creatures, and think of the many people like it, dependent on others because they are small or crippled or blind, dependent because they are poor, not able to choose where they will live, how they will live, where they will go, what they will do; like Christ in the host, in other people's hands.

Which (using imperfect human language) was Christ's most effective moment of love? When was he doing most to redeem humanity? Surely when he was helpless on the cross. It is in our futility that we, in whom Christ lives, live his supreme moment of effective love, the moment of the consummation of his love on the cross.

Now think . . . my hands, unskilled, clumsy, Christ's hands which raised the dead, nailed back, helpless. My narrow apostolate, the one street, the one room, the one office, Christ's feet nailed down to one plank of wood. My want of words, failure to express myself, Christ's tongue black and swollen, dumb in the silence of death. My heart, ridiculous in its futile, unsatisfied love, Christ's heart broken open, a little piece of clay.

Sacrifice and oblation thou wouldst not, but a body thou hast fitted to me; then said I, Behold I come, in the head of the book it is written of me, that I should do thy will, O God.

Then there are our own hands. Some people have the supreme offering of pain, they are able to contemplate Christ crucified in every nerve and fibre. The old carvers of the twelfth century understood that, they carved the ribs hard and straight round the sacred body like five fingers of pain, gripping and constricting the heart. They also often carved the hands with the fingers curled lovingly round nails, looking almost like the hands of children holding their treasures as they fall asleep—as if our pain fastening him to us for ever were Christ's treasure. Some can make the prayer of the body most real to themselves by offering it all through their hands, hands which so perfectly express life. All day this offering through the hands goes on, in the cooking and sweeping, in wringing out the washing-up mop, in bathing the children, sewing their clothes, typing, writing, digging, nursing the sick. Think too of artists' hands, surgeons' hands and the hands of masseures, the hands of little children struggling laboriously with chalk and pencils, the hands of artisans' apprentices dedicated to the discipline of acquiring skill, and hands making the sign of the cross. But it is all the sign of the cross, all the fingers of Christ curled lovingly on the nails.

THE PRECIOUS OINTMENT

If we find religion depressing it is because our conception of Christ is narrow and conventional. We do not perceive the sensitiveness of his human nature, the poet and the lover in him. If we did, and if we looked for these qualities in Christ in our neighbour, we would discover subtleties and depths of beauty in people who seemed quite uninteresting before.

Most of us instinctively recognise Christ in outcasts, in the poor man and the afflicted, and we can thank God for it, but we seldom recognise him in those of our own household. After two thousand years with us, living under the same roof, sharing our fireside, sitting at our table, Christ may well repeat his sad, patient words spoken on the night before he died: 'Here am I, who have been all this while in your company: hast thou not learned to recognise me yet?'

No contemplation makes life so radiant as the contemplation of Christ in one another. The prayer breaking out from it should be extravagance, poetry, a carefree uncalculating grace in our personal relationships.

In sharp contrast to this, many people today think that the only justification for religion at all is that it be utility religion. As little of it as possible, they say, costing as little as possible, strictly utilitarian, and this they apply even to our love of Christ in our neighbour. Outward puritanism is repressed nowadays in a welter of paganism, but there is an inward puritanism, yet uglier, which mistrusts supernatural joy and condemns loveliness in loving.

I know a charitable woman who sacrifices her coupons to clothe poor children, but she will clothe them only in grey cloth. Poor little Christ child, who wore gaily striped benoozies and delighted in the iridescent dresses of the wild lilies, now clothed in grey, because he is still poor!

Christ does not change. He accepted the gifts of the magi, gold, frankincense and myrrh, he accepted the crown, too heavy for his little head to wear. He was grateful for the waste of spikenard poured over his feet. Our thoughts close like a wing, silent in this thought, that God was grateful to a public sinner for an act of courtesy that proved her understanding of his sensitive heart.

He spoke as a poet, called himself 'light'. His symbols were wheat and vines, the fig tree breaking into leaf, burning candles. To give us his life, he used water and bread and wine. Through the mouth of John he said: 'I will give you the morning star'. Could anything be more beautiful, less utilitarian?

God is not niggardly, he does not give only what is useful or necessary, he does not clothe his children in grey cloth. Everything that he gives us for our life has its own particular beauty. He gives as a lover gives. His gifts must delight our senses as well as our souls. His healing herbs smell sweet. He gives overflowingly and to everyone. Look at the river of stars in the milky way, the multitudinous grass and corn, the squander of seeds flung down the wind for every tree that takes root! 'Come', he says, 'you who are thirsty, take you who will, the water of life is my free gift!'

If we recognise Christ in everyone and bring this lyrical expression of love to him in daily life, we shall do away with the monotony and drabness, the sense of inferiority that dogs so many people today. We must be uncalculating, spending everything we have joyfully on the loveliness of living and giving life, bringing poetry into everything, into our words and gestures, setting the table, for meals, bringing flowers into the house, making love visible, tangible, audible.

Deny it as we will, there is a terrible endemic discouragement among us. The practice of this contemplation would bring reassurance and new life, like the sun suddenly shining through clouds. In that light, minds that were grey and dull would put out tender shoots and flower, like dry wood at the touch of the warm sun.

Such too is the spirit of the church, manifest through the centuries in her liturgy and her cathedrals lifting their flowering steeples to the stars, standing in their moats of meadow grass, with the offerings of kings and peasants, of the magi and the shepherds down the centuries, gold and linen and oil and light, music and gesture and wine and wheat and flowers, brought to Christ's feet.

The secret of knowing is loving. Those who love Christ, know the heart of God that was grateful for the lovely extravagance that made a sinner break her box of precious ointment over his feet. It seemed sheer waste to Judas, but immediately Christ made the waste of love part of the eternal treasure of his death. 'She has done it for my burial'. Christ made it one thing for ever with the expression of love that would illumine the common life, with the tenderness of the saints shedding their tears upon his feet, with the sacrifice of the loveliest, that is scandal to the world.

It is the participation of lyrical love in Christ's passion. It is the sacrifice, when occasion arises, of the thing that is good in itself, and could be holy in itself; the sacrifice of the newly married conscript's home, of the young soldier's love that will never be consummated, of his child who will never be born, of his dreams that will never be tarnished by realisation.

It is the breaking open of the human heart to pour out the sheer sweetness of life over the feet of Christ for his burial.

THE TOMB

The modern world is the tomb of Christ. Sometimes we feel inclined to echo the question of the mourners in Jerusalem: 'Who is to roll the stone away for us?', so heavy are the circumstances which seem to prevent the resurrection we long for.

Faith is our most urgent need today. Not vague aspirations, but clear-cut, definite faith in what Christ said. Faith that we can follow like a map. For many the meaning of the word is forgotten. Some imagine that they have faith because though they doubt the virgin birth, they enjoy Christmas carols; some because they hope confusedly for a christian state with higher wages and no restriction on individual sin.

To work, to hope, to live for less than complete christianity, to accept a compromise, to lose confidence in man's capacity for goodness, is to deny our faith.

Christ has faith in man. He said that he was salt, giving savour to life that would be flat and tasteless without him. He said that he was the light of the world, burning out across the darkness. He said that he would make his own home in man's soul and even make him one with God the Father. If that is Christ's faith in man, we must at least believe in the potential Christ in every man alive.

We must have faith in Christ in the tomb of the sinner's soul. The Russian pilgrims, driven by an impulse as mysterious as the migration of birds, left all that they had to go on foot to Jerusalem. There they prostrated themselves with tears of adoring joy and kissed the cold stone of the empty sepulchre. Yet that is an empty tomb. In the soul of the sinner the dead Christ lies covered in his wounds, waiting for us to come, looking for him there and bringing, not condemnation, but balm to anoint his body.

If we judge by the newspapers, it would seem that christianity is a failure. Famine, cruelty, suspicion, threats, fear, violence, crime. This after two thousand years of christianity! Certainly it looks like a failure. What did it look like when Christ was in the tomb? Christ had claimed to be the life of the world—he was dead. He had promised his people a kingdom, he had been hanged outside the city. He had claimed to be king, he had been crowned with thorns. Only a handful of men had kept their faith in him and the handful had fled. One of them had even denied that he knew him, another had sold him for a contemptible fee. He was stripped naked, made mock of, he died with nothing of his own, even his grave was borrowed. Certainly it looked as if Christ was a failure.

At that time the faith of the whole world was kept alive by a few devoted women. Even the apostles doubted them when they told them (what they should have known) that

Christ had kept his word. 'But to their minds the story seemed madness and they could not believe it'.

Those women believed it because they had the faith which discovers through love. They had never wanted any earthly triumph for Christ, never expected it. They believed in Christ the poor man, the forsaken man, even the crucified man. If they could not have Christ with all his humiliations and stripes, they would not seek to comfort themselves with anything else. So they came, asking who would roll back the stone, to find it already removed and Christ alive, with the wounds our sin had inflicted on him blazing like stars in his risen body.

Today it is in the Catholic church that faith in the resurrection is kept alive. Often enough too some pious old woman is the keeper of the church's faith, faith that is nourished by intimate personal love for the suffering Christ—the very tender love that seeks for Christ, crucified in man.

For a time when he was dead there was no visible sign that Christ had ever lived, other than the empty cross, but from that cross he had sown the hidden seed of his life, from that seed in the full cycle of his love resurrection would come, not from above like ideology, but from right down in the darkness of man's being. Not with splendour, but secretly as the coming of bread into the wheat.

Christ's dereliction was public. His whole world saw and was scandalised. His resurrection was as secret as the dew. Today we have seen the passion, we have seen the crucifiction and dereliction, now our faith must be faith in mankind crucified or it is not faith at all.

Our generation of martyrs have sown the seed of Christ's blood from their own veins, dyeing their native soil crimson with his life. Can we doubt his resurrection in those lands—in Russia, Spain, Germany, Mexico and Poland? It would be mockery to be exalted by the accounts of the deaths of our martyrs if we do not believe in the fertility of their blood.

Faith in the crucified Christ is faith in the risen. The world may never recognise his kingdom, for it will always be a secret in the soul, never an outward show of power. The love that goes looking for Christ in the tomb, that believes in him in all men, embalms him in sinners, trusts him in martyrs, follows him in the footsteps of the derelict and the afflicted, that love will see him risen and will acknowledge him as king, without trying to whittle down a single thorn in his crown of thorns. They will keep the faith of the world. Meantime his own question is our most fitting act of faith: 'Was it not to be expected that Christ should undergo these sufferings, and enter so into his glory?'

THE RISEN LIFE

Christ's risen life, shown during the forty days between the resurrection and the ascension is the pattern for our life in him. It is in the risen life that we live: we can accept his passion in our own lives only because he who lives our life in us has 'overcome the world'. He has suffered all that we shall ever suffer, he has even died each of our deaths, and he has overcome death.

At first sight the most astonishing thing about the risen life is its ordinariness. But that is wholly consistent with Christ's way. His revelation of himself was always gradual, always told like a secret. Before knowing him as God, he wanted men to know him as themselves, so that they would not be afraid to come close to him. Now he is determined that his incredible experience of having died and come back shall not make a barrier. There must be no sense of the uncanny to awe his apostles.

He will not even startle them by letting them realise suddenly, unwarned, that he is there. They must first realise that they are with someone ordinary, and afterwards learn who it is. His greeting is always a reassurance. He is concerned by so human a thing as whether they have something savoury to make their dry bread palatable. He lights a fire and cooks a little breakfast for them himself. His way of making his identity known shows how well he knew 'what was in the heart of man'. He knew what each individual needed to make their share in the joy of his resurrection possible.

Peter is not asked to say that he is sorry, only to reassure himself and Christ that he really does love him in spite of those denials. It is a fact that makes the mind dumb with wonder that Christ always wanted to be reassured of people's love. It mattered more to him than anything they had done to wrong him, in fact nothing else mattered at all. Magdalene knew him by the mingled tenderness and restraint with which he greeted her; both things were her dire need. Thomas, the forerunner of all those who do not agree that seeing is believing, must touch the wounds in his body. The disciples going to Emmaus were first given light on the whole subject of Christ's suffering, light that glowed within them. Afterwards they knew him in the breaking of bread.

Our life is sacramental. We do not live that peculiar thing one hears so much of, a 'spiritual life'. We live a natural and a supernatural life, we live it through the medium of the simplest substance of things. Our Lord gave himself to us through our flesh and blood, we give ourselves back to him through it. The symbols of the gift of his own life are bread, wine, water and oil. We give our life back to him through the dust he made us out of, through everything we see and touch and taste and hear, the food we eat, the clothes we wear, the words we speak, the sleep we sleep. Such are the sacramentals of our love, things ordinary with the ordinariness of the risen Christ.

Our apostolic life, and not to be apostolic is not to be christian, is just as ordinary. Our communion with one another, which is our Christ-giving to one another, is in eating, working, sharing the common sorrows and responsibilities, comforting one another in soul and body, talking to one another.

The Catholic church has a secret to reveal. The church is not only the hierarchy but all the people, sinners as much as saints, foolish and wise, the young, the mature, the old, little children, rich and poor, strong and weak. All of us. The secret is, Christ risen lives in us. Certainly he has continued his policy of not letting his identity be obvious! We must copy his way if anyone is ever to recognise him.

The secret must be told not by aggressive propaganda but by learning the needs of other people's souls and answering them from ours, giving them as much of the secret as they can at present bear, in the way that they individually can receive it—an effacing of self that is a revelation of Christ. To some we may reveal him by cooking and serving a meal, by a little concern about whether in these days they can enjoy their food, the meal on the shore. To some by accepting their expression of love: 'Peter lovest thou me?' To some by tenderness that restrains, Magdalene in the garden. To others by showing them their own wounds in our lives, Thomas. To yet others by telling them the doctrine of suffering, and by giving them Christ's passion through reparation, the disciples at Emmaus.

If we could imagine the first Easter, the moment of reunion between Christ and his Father, that would be already heaven. The world saw only the empty cross, stark against the dawn, but the glory of the resurrection had begun secretly in the human heart. Today the world sees the cross as something empty and stark against the doubtful grey dawn of a doubtful new era. The glory is still secret, but it is a secret that is communicated to millions, through the simplest substances of life and the hourly practice of love. Resurrection is in the hearts of those who love, the heart of Christ beginning to beat in them.

EASTER

There is no desire that returns so inevitably and so often to human nature as the desire to be made new. That is why we rejoice in spring as we do. In some inexplicable way we partake of the newness of the earth, our own hearts are quickened by it and after the numbness of the frozen winter they wake to a lyrical, even a virginal capacity for joy.

So too with dawn. After those seemingly interminable nights that we all experience at some time or other, nights of grief or pain, the coming of light brings hope and courage, as if the daybreak was happening inside our hearts. We depend, perhaps more than we realise, on rhythm, on the circles flowing from darkness to light, from seeding to flowering, from death to birth, on the rhythm that is both outside us, all round us and within us.

Joy, love, hope, those things which in the natural order enable us continually to overcome the everyday stress and sorrow of life, to take up the cross daily without undue sadness, are not given to us once and for all, to be locked up and kept hidden and hoarded in us like precious gems in a casket. They by their nature must be continually renewed, and like creative energy they are renewed only by being spent. It is precisely because they fill the heart only when it has been emptied out that though we expect their return instinctively as the ear expects the repetition in music, and hence even their absence makes us hope, the sweetness of their returning always keeps its quality of astonishment. Their potency is in their newness.

It seems a law of fallen nature that life must always come to its being through darkness, and this makes us even more aware of its beauty. Dawn is lovelier because it comes after night, spring because it follows the winter.

All this is but the dim shadow of the law of our mysterious life in Christ. On Easter Sunday, all over the world, a cry goes up, *Lumen Christi*—'Light of Christ'. Everywhere new fire is kindled. Christ has risen, after the dark night of his passion he is the morning light, after the cold darkness of the tomb he is the white bloom on the thorn. His resurrection is not something far away, merely remembered in the church's radiant liturgy. It is Christ dawning, Christ flowering in our lives, now, today. That is what Easter means: man has his heart's desire, he is made new, new with the newness of the risen Christ, burning with the new fire of his love.

This Easter in the heart happens in a natural way, not in the violent fashion of a revivalist conversion. It is as secret as the miracle of flowering. Children have been known to sit watching buds hopefully for hours, but they never see them opening. Only suddenly they *have* opened, the flower is there! Easter in us is not something that happens once and is ended, Christ makes us new not only once but over and over again.

The seed sown on Calvary comes into flower in generation after generation, in life after life, and over and over again in each life the wood of the cross blossoms with the white flower of Christ. We can accept whatever suffering comes to us as the certain beginning of joy.

As often as we surrender our wills to suffering in any form in which it comes into our lives, Christ will follow it. We can repeat our Lord's prayer at the beginning of the vast circle of love he was to tread through death to life: 'thy will be done', not dreading the darkness but rejoicing in the joy that must follow it, because God's ultimate will for us is our joy.

When sorrow comes we shall readily surrender ourselves to it, with minds as quiet as sleep. Indeed we shall surrender our wills as children do to sleep when darkness comes, waiting untroubled for the day they cannot hasten, certain that it will come to waken them with its light. Meantime they sleep, safe in the home built round them by their father's love. We too can give our minds to rest in darkness, knowing that 'under us are the eternal arms'.

The first Easter was the waking of the Son of God from the

sleep of death. All our Easters are awakenings, when self has died and the repose of surrender is accomplished. The heart wakes to awareness of life's loveliness in the light of Christ. With his light illuminating the mind everything is seen clearly with true vision. Suffering itself is seen as it really is for the first time, as an indispensable part of the rhythm of joy, and we listen to the words of the Easter liturgy with new understanding: 'This is the night of which it is written: and the night shall be enlightened as the day and the night is my light in my enjoyments'.

At the heart of that liturgy is the wonder of life, life symbolised in the selfless purity of water, blessed and bidden to flow into every corner of the earth, irrigating and making fruitful the dry dust of humanity, new fire burning to kindle the human heart with Christ's love, new incense to carry it up to him in adoration, and light, the light of Christ within us, giving us our heart's desire, making us new. The sun of eternal love, radiating now from within our own hearts, renewing the earth: 'Lo! I make all things new'.

A Note on Suffering

Today every sensitive person is shocked by the sight of suffering, or more accurately by the sight of evil suddenly made visible. The evils that we see today have always existed—fear, slavery, hunger, destitution, disease, frustration, death—but it is only lately that we have had to live face to face with them. Before they were more or less hidden or covered up. War has forced us to meet them daily in the open, sometimes in humanity, sometimes in our friends, sometimes in our own hearts.

Because of this many in bewilderment turn against God. They say 'There is no God', as if this could ease their anguish. One asks 'Would suffering really be easier if there were no God?' Would poverty be less hard if we did not believe that we have an eternal Father who knows our needs? Would loneliness if we did not believe in the nearness of one to whom the secrets of our hearts are known? Or death if we were sure that death is the end, and that no unimaginable love waits to enfold the dead to the heart of life?

Astonishing though it is, the answer is 'Yes'. Many people would find these things easier to endure, or anyhow more easy to contemplate in others, if there were no God; or at all events they sincerely imagine that they would for they would be free of the aggravating bitterness of resentment against a person. A person whom they are asked to accept as all-powerful and all-loving, and who yet allows the agony of the world.

Rightly nothing makes those without faith, or with

tottering faith, angrier than the person who tries to dispose of the mystery of suffering by slick argument, winding up with an exhortation and promise of abstract benefits to be derived from a complacent attitude to the pain of humanity. The unfathomable darkness of suffering can only be briefly lit here and there by the light of God as he reveals his light, never by human wisdom. At the point where the light of God touches a human being healing begins, not only for the individual, but through him for the whole world. The only service that one who by God's mercy alone holds the faith can offer, is to restate, as simply as he can, what God has revealed, what the church does teach about the secret of suffering.

First of all the very bitterness of the revolt, far from proving that there is not a God, proves that there is one; it is certainly not evoked by nothing—by no one. It is because God's power is recognised, if not admitted, that his claim to be Love is resented so bitterly.

'Love'—that is the word on which everything turns . . . if there is one thing in which men *do* believe, in which nothing can shatter their faith, it is love. Of course the word is continually abused and much is called love that is not, but in their heart of hearts all men know the real thing from its travesty, and they value it more than life.

To say that someone is incapable of love is equal to saying that he is sub-human, and for a man to realise this in himself would be the greatest imaginable humiliation. No amount of virtue could make a saint of one wanting in love; love is the heartbeat of sanctity, without it virtue is dead. On the other hand the whole world forgives any sin or failure in one who proves his great capacity for love. So did the Lord of the world. There is no experience comparable to that which we call 'being in love'. It is only through it that we discover the glory and sweetness of the flowering of our own life.

Ask any young man in love if the suffering that he has known is worth the hour that it has brought him to, or if he would now forego his love to be exempt from future sorrow. It is not necessary for me to tell you his answer.

Suppose that God gave every man the choice between a world in which there was no suffering, but also no capacity for love, or a world in which suffering remains, but everyone has the power to love. Which do you think mankind would choose? Which would *you* choose? Quite certainly the power to love, even at the cost of suffering.

Now this is precisely what has happened. The thing which makes us able to love is free-will, and it is the same thing, free-will, which makes us able to sin. Without it there would be no sin and no love in the world.

Suffering is the result of sin. It is not God who allows it, it is you and I. God did not give us our free-will to sin with, but to love with. Loneliness, poverty, sickness, death, these things are not God's will but against it. They are the things, they and all the other agonies of human nature, that *we* consent to when we sin.

But as we have brought suffering into the world, God does all he can, without taking away our free-will, and so taking away our humanity, to change suffering from something that crushes and destroys us into something that exalts and renews us. This is a miracle which could be effected only by absolute love, and beside which the creation of the world is pale.

There is one characteristic of this generation that is wholly good, our growing realisation of human solidarity, of our need for one another, the real oneness of all human creatures. Perhaps this realisation is the seed that has been sown in secret by all the nameless martyrs of this century. True it is often wrongly manifested and misunderstood, as indeed it must be while there are millions who do not know God, but like a seed it is striving and pushing through darkness to light, and in the light we hope.

Today only those who are less than human want to live to themselves. The average man, however dimly he yet sees his way, wants to be part of the whole of humanity, one of the human family. He wants his life to be part of the world's resurrection. Perhaps in this stirring of his heart, there is the beginning of the answer to our Lord's prayer for the world, 'that they may all be one'.

But our consciousness of our oneness with all men will only become the vital communion of love that it should be when each one of us bravely accepts his personal responsibility for the suffering of the world. We are as much one in this as we are in hope. In practice, every sin we commit adds to the sum of the world's sorrow, every act of love mitigates it. Suffering, if we are one with Christ and so offer it in his hands to God, is the most effective of all acts of love.

This is not a fanciful idea, it can be a reality. Christ is the incarnation of love itself. Love itself become flesh and blood, become our flesh and blood, therefore with our suffering, with our pain and sorrow. He did not bring suffering into the world, but because we had done so and it was there, he came to wed himself to it, to make it inseparable from his redeeming love, one thing with love itself.

By making our humanity one with his, by making our suffering his own, he has literally given himself to us, made his suffering ours, so that we now have as our own his power of love. His sacrifice offered for the world is irresistible to the Father. Because it is real reparation for sin it lightens the heavy burden that is bending the back of humanity, and man can lift himself up. In it the world's healing begins.

It is this power of his own love that Christ has given to us. Because of it our personal share in the world's suffering is never useless, always potent. It is the most effective gift we have for the good of our fellow men.

In Christ all humanity is contained. If we live in him we can lift up all the world's suffering in our own, and we can bear this mystery without staggering because of the miraculous economy of pity, through which in each man's suffering *all* suffering can be turned to love, but no one man can suffer more than his one heart's measure of grief.

It is *only* the God who is love who can bring light to the dark secret of human sorrow. When that light shines upon it, it is seen as the supreme communion of Christ's love between men. The measure in which our own suffering becomes love is not the size of our suffering, but the degree of our oneness with Christ.

Poverty

If Christ's teaching about poverty had done nothing else, it
would at least have kept man's wit alive, for men—and still
more, women—have used all their ingenuity for centuries to
wriggle out of it. They assure you that if you are 'poor in
spirit' you may be as rich in body as you like. All that is
required is that you are indifferent to (and therefore
presumably ungrateful for) your wealth. Thus it is merely a
happy chance which causes you to wander into the Savoy for
lunch when you would like Lyon's Corner House equally
well.

That, being at all events on the lavish side, is a pleasing
evasion; equally popular as a conception of holy poverty is
meanness, allowing others to foot the bill every time, even to
providing the stamps for the letters you write to them. That
is sometimes just canonised meanness, and sometimes a worse
thing, namely a thin sanctimonious disguise for being
ashamed of the real poverty that should be honoured. These,
and all other substitutes for Christ's poverty, show not the
spirit of poverty but poverty of the spirit; they are the very
opposite to the poverty of the saints. They, the saints,
different in so many things, have all been alike in one thing—
all without exception have had the spirit of poverty.

The poverty of Christ is not destitution, though actually
Christ was destitute for part of his life, and in every age one
or more of the saints have had a true vocation for absolute
poverty. Such saints are St John the Baptist, St Francis of
Assisi, St Joseph Benedict Labré. For such a vocation there
is room in modern life. So falsified are all our standards that

we are inclined to forget that there is any such thing as intrinsic value. Our money in England is made of paper. Maybe a lot of children do not even know that each note represents a golden coin, and that if the coin did not exist the paper would be worth nothing; probably many children alive now have never set eyes on a golden sovereign. Saints who are chosen by God to be destitute, to have literally nothing, are the pure gold that shows us that holy poverty has an intrinsic value.

There was an old man who called at his bank every week and asked to see his money in gold. 'I like to see what I have got', he explained. We christians have 'got' Christ's absolute poverty. Although we are allowed to have reasonable comfort ourselves, the grace and power of Christ's real destitution belongs to us. His homelessness, his nakedness, his loneliness, the poverty of the dead man on the cross, all that belongs to us as christians, and in times of crisis we can draw on it. At all times we can rely on it, without it the gentler poverty would have no value and we should be a spiritually bankrupt race.

The grace of Christ's utter poverty is given to all the destitute and homeless people in the world, outcasts and refugees; without it, they would despair. Any one of us at any time now may need to draw on this pure gold of Christ's poverty. From time to time, like the old man, we want to see what we have got. Those saints who baffle the faithless by leading lives which seem to them to be useless, even selfish, lives like Christ's public life, poorer than the wild foxes and the birds, show us that his poverty is still our wealth, is still triumphant. Even in human nature as it is today, Christ, naked and foolish on the cross, can be king.

Poverty, not destitution, the simpler poverty which many people experience, makes us more sensitive, more selective, able to perceive the poetry in life. Riches, on the other hand, blunt the soul and the senses. It is true that sometimes a rich person can be saved, sometimes they can use money for their

own and other people's joy, and can live with the wisdom
that makes life lovely, but when this happens it is, as Christ
has said, a miracle, and it happens as rarely as a miracle.

The general rule is otherwise. To be rich is to live in an
overcrowded house, a house of life overcrowded with false
values; they encumber like useless heirlooms. They ought to
be thrown out of the windows but the courage and the
virility to do this are lacking. There are the family traditions,
as conventional and stupid as Cousin Martha's water-
colours, which must be kept until she dies; the family
snobbery inherited from Great-grandpa and as ugly as his
portrait which takes up so much space but must be kept in
order not to offend Grandmother. There is Aunt Amy's
prudery, which like the flower vase she gave us won't hold
water because it is cracked but has to be displayed for the
same reason. There are the countless vanities and prejudices
that our own circle of acquaintances and hangers-on have
persuaded us to accept, together with the spate of whimsical
and futile ornaments which give our tables, desks and
mantelpieces a kind of rash of breakables, and finally the
worry and anxiety of it all which is so like the valuable
spindle-legged chairs that give such an appearance of good
taste but which would collapse at once if we sat on them too
heavily.

How wonderful to dare to make a bonfire of it all! But
there is central heating in good houses, and besides cracking
the walls, it enervates, so we can't.

Poverty is like one room. The windows are open, the sun
comes in, the walls are whitewashed, there are one or two
books chosen for our delight, they are read and re-read; if
there is a picture it is one bought at the cost of sacrifice
because it is a real joy, we see it because there is no bric-a-
brac to distract from it. There is one earthenware pot that
holds water, and the wild flowers know in it their affinity to
earth and rain. This room is a workroom, in it we learn the
joy of good work, done well, and of the real charity, the

fellow-feeling, of working with others. We share the dreams, the ardours and the endurances of other people; we have the key to love.

'Blessed are the poor in spirit', says Christ, 'For theirs is the kingdom of heaven'. This is true, all the other beatitudes promise future blessedness, but this one gives the loveliest of all, here and now, the kingdom of heaven, which in this life is known in the wonder and the realisation of life and beauty, in the keenness of the mind and of the senses, in the power of selection and in the response of the unspoilt spirit to God and man.

The Mass and the Missions

It is estimated that in every second of the day and night four elevations of the host take place. I never cease to wonder at this, or to rejoice in the knowledge that there is never a second of one's life in which one cannot lift up one's heart to God in the heart of Christ lifted up in the host.

I think, too, of all the places in the world where the mass is being celebrated; of how Christ, who began his earthly life in a stable and ended it on a scaffold, has penetrated into every place and circumstance of human life, and has gathered every fragment of man's love to be offered in sacrifice.

Think of all the places where mass is being celebrated at this present moment, the very moment in which you are reading this page; all the cathedrals and all the churches of the world, all the tin huts and mud huts and make-shifts that are the best man can do in many mission fields and in English villages, robbed by the reformation of their little Saxon churches. In ships out on the deep seas, on battlefields and camps, in prisons and hospital wards, in the desert and the jungle, in the great cities of the world, in the cottages of faithful peasants in persecuted countries, and under the tall trees of lonely forests of exile.

Think too how everywhere where Christ is lifted up men are bowed down in adoration, soldiers, sailors, airmen, fishermen, men of every country, of every colour, rich men and poor men, free men and prisoners, old men and young men, men of every craft and trade and profession, all adoring God, all in communion with one another, all in communion with the Holy Father, all in communion with you and me.

'And I, if I be lifted up, will draw all men to me'.

It was during the London blitz that the glory of this
ceaseless elevation came home to me as never before. It was
often difficult then to hear mass, or to be able to receive
communion. Of course mass was offered daily, but there were
many things to hinder and sometimes to frustrate our efforts
to get to it. Fantastic hours of duty, day and night, sirens and
bombing that forced one to take cover again and again on
the way, and finally the possibility, too often realised, of
finding a ruin where last night there was a church.

In those days I learnt for ever how thankful one should be
for being able to hear mass easily, even when 'easily' means
a long country walk on a dark winter's morning.

Now more than a year after the end of the war I still
experience a sense of relief like a load falling from the heart
every time I go to mass, and over and over again on the way
I think of those others who still have, and may always have,
dangers and hardships to face in order to go to mass. Of
martyrs and potential martyrs in persecuted countries, of
missionaries who endure any privation, any risk, to take
Christ to the ends of the earth to be adored, to give him, as
the bread of life, to any little spiritual starveling in pagan
lands, who but for the church would count for nothing in
the world's eyes, but who in the eyes of the church is worth
the shedding of Christ's blood on the cross and the lives of the
martyrs given that his blood should flow for them in the
chalice.

If someone with the knowledge to do it would write a book
about the price that gallant men and women have paid
gladly to hear mass all through the ages, from the time of the
catacombs until now in all the countries of the world, what
an inspiration that would be! How it would shame us when
we do not go to mass simply because it would mean a little
effort which we are too lazy to make.

In our days stories of the mass, penetrating in their beauty and heroism, come to us from many parts of the world, where to celebrate mass may easily cost a priest's life. Strange lovely whispers come from Siberia of mass offered on a felled tree and a little stone from the ground for altar, and the celebrant, a venerable bishop, dancing in the snow for joy, at the *Ite Missa Est*. Again of a little wine, frozen in a wooden cup, which had to be melted over the priest's heart before it could be changed into the precious blood.

And while these stories fill our hearts there are countless others, seldom told because they are not new but agelong, of the constant fight with burning heat and bitter cold, with paganism often as murderous as communism, with vast distances, with witchcraft and sinister voiceless hostilities, with martyrdoms sometimes as searching to a man's soul as death, isolation, exile, aridity, and on the human plane unimaginable loneliness.

To the Holy Father all these missionaries are always present. His heart goes out to them and his heart is the heart of their shepherd, there is not one lonely young pioneer, not one old missionary shrivelled by scorching suns and feeling himself to be of no account, whom the pope does not cherish with the love of a shepherd and a father. He himself offers mass for them at that altar in Rome which is the centre and heart of humanity. Receiving our Lord's body and blood in communion he communicates with them too, and with their flocks. And he communicates with us too, kneeling at our own altar rails, offering our mass in union with him for the missions.

Now in the wells of our bombed churches wild flowers grow. There is a purple flower, so delicate that it looks life drifts of cloud in the grass. It has come to be known to Londoners as the 'flower of the ruins' and a symbol of resurrection. Now when I pass it on my way to mass I am reminded of the courage and the suffering that many endure today that mass may be offered from sunrise to sunset everywhere, and of the missionaries and martyrs all through history, of their long journeys in little sailing vessels over bitter seas, through overgrown, trackless country, over vast plains, into deep forests, journeys made with the same object as my easy one today, that Christ be adored, that Christ be received everywhere.

All these saints and martyrs are here with me at my local altar, and here with me is the pope and all the christians in the world. No wonder it is my delight, as well as a point of honour, to offer mass for our missions, and to lift up my heart many times a day with the ceaseless elevation of the host. 'Lift up your hearts' is the reminder of the wild flowers in the ruins, and our answer: 'We have, to the Lord'.

Christmas 1945

I once overheard a remark which started me thinking about Christmas in a new way. Until then I had seen it through the medium of the Christmas card, Christmas roses and snow and a plentiful sprinkle of glitter-frost that we could buy then at 2d a packet. The remark which made me begin to think was 'There must have been mice and spiders in the stable at Bethlehem'. Yes, Christ was born not into a fanciful world, but into our real world that includes mice and spiders.

Read the gospels for Christmas and you will see the likeness between Christ's day and ours. It is almost shocking. You recognise Herod, the murder of the innocents, the flight into Egypt, the homeless refugees in a strange land, the young mother trudging from door to door, seeking somewhere to give birth to her baby, and posted on every door in Bethlehem the notice, so familiar to us, 'No rooms to let'.

The likeness is also in the minds of men. Christ came into a world sickened with persecution, obsessed with fear. Those who waited for him expected an earthly kingdom, they wanted power to match with power.

It is as hard for most people today to believe in the littleness, the humility of Christ, as it would have been for the Jews in his own day to believe that the shivering baby, born like a poor little bleating lamb out in the dark and the cold, could set them free.

Obsessed by the struggle for temporal existence we forget that man is both soul and body, that peace is not something that this world can give. We forget that such things as wonder and poetry and prayer are as much our needs as food and drink and sleep. We profess christianity but are almost shocked by it in practice, so complacently have we accepted a utility religion of materialism, security, good health.

We want Christ on our terms, Christ gives himself only on his own. He is purity, truth, humility, simplicity, love.

In him is the wholeness of man, soul and body, the kingdom of heaven in the heart, the peace that the world cannot give. By him the simplest materials of life become the substance of eternal love. He does not despise them, he takes them into his hands: in his hands, bread is changed to God.

Our souls are like the inn, crowded, noisy, restless. We herd together to try to forget that we are afraid, we almost literally shout our hearts down. We shrink from the silence that must fall upon our souls if they are to cradle the child of burning snow.

Nevertheless we must find that point of stillness today, because it is Christmas and Christmas means one thing and one thing only, that it is the divine will of love to be born in our hearts. Christmas 1945 is the birth of Christ in us.

He is the word of God, telling the forgotten secret of infinite love once more. He wants to tell it in our voices and in our words.

I used to think how vexed the innkeeper would have been had he found out who it was that he had turned from his door, but I have learnt to think that thankfulness would have overcome vexation, because after all he had the quiet, dark stable just outside and he had lent that to the peasant girl in whom God was hidden.

Anyway it was Christ himself who chose the stable to be born in. He still chooses unlikely places. In each of us, just beyond the noise of our outward life, there is some place of silence and darkness, an emptiness where, if we have courage enough, we are alone with ourselves. There in this place of silence, we know that God alone can fill our emptiness, he alone can content us, he alone is our peace.

It is in this secret place of the soul that Christ wants to be born in us. He wants to be born in us, that through us he may live in this world again and make it new with his new life. Make it young with his youngness, little with his littleness, true with his truth, childlike with his childhood, pure with his purity.

It is in this dark place of our heart that Christ wants the light of the world to begin to burn and from its burning to radiate, until it shines back from the face of humanity. Here it is that he wants the light to begin to shine in darkness and the life of the world to begin again.

In him there was life and the life was the light of men, and the light shines in darkness that was not able to master it.

It is easy to see that the world is wounded, hard to see that its healing begins in our own heart. We say, repeatedly and rather pompously, that only a vital christianity can save the world, but how do we imagine that a vital christianity begins? I have heard it said, like an infection—that it could come as an epidemic, a sort of theological influenza, that we could sneeze on to one another in spasms of fervour. But that surely would pass like influenza, leaving weakness if nothing worse. Vital christianity means a living Christhood, a living Christ in man's heart, and Christ can live in our hearts only if he is born in them individually. He can be born in us only if we accept him in his own way, in littleness, humility, secret, hidden and small, to be fostered and loved in us, cradled and clothed in us, that he may grow naturally in our lives to his full stature.

It requires faith to believe that Christ will be born in man this Christmas, but much more faith to believe that he will be born in our own heart, that he could fulfil his will of love in our own life, our life with so little radius for his light, so little journeying for his feet, so small a distance for his hands to reach, and such constriction round his heart.

Our life is too small, too mediocre. Perhaps, despite our complaining, when we face the facts squarely, there is not even much suffering in it. How could Christ, the redeemer, the crucified, live again in us?

Christ chose the stable, the narrowness, the secrecy, as if he had bound up his own omnipotence in swaddling bands. People passing the door could never have guessed that anything was happening inside, that God was being born in there! And who knew? About six men out of the whole world, two or three shepherds who heard the singing of angels, three mysterious scholars, who followed the stars. They all come silently out of the darkness, kneel for a moment and are gone again. We see them no more, nor hear their voices. They knew that they had seen the Lord, but seem not to have told anyone else. A child smiled on them in the night, that is all we know of them. And soon the child himself fled away from Bethlehem and disappeared from our sight.

Now he comes to be born in the narrowness of our lives, to be incarnate in us, to give his love to the world through us, through our flesh and blood. That is one meaning of the incarnation.

The reason why we are where we are this Christmas, in this house, family, office, workroom, hospital or camp, is because it is here in this place that Christ wants to be born, from here that he wants his life to begin again in the world.

The reason why we are with these particular people is because it is precisely to these people that Christ wants us to give his love. This year we are his trustees for these people, he has put his love for them into our hands, into our hearts. We did not choose this place—Christ has chosen it. We did not choose these people—Christ has chosen them.

We are asked one thing, to have the humility and courage to open the secret place of our heart to Christ, conscious though we are that it is as derelict as the stable, and that his light will reveal the mouse and the spider.

It may have been puzzling, even to Mary, how Christ was giving his life to the whole world in the obscurity of

Bethlehem, but enough for her that this was his way. It still is, and he himself is the way, the only way to our peace.

Because the Word of God was humble as the bleating of a lamb, lost along the darkness, today the voices of men and angels are a great choir singing in the light, 'Lamb of God, you take away the sin of the world, give us peace'.

The Care of the Mentally Ill

Among the wonders of God's love, that which seems to me most to reveal his tenderness for men is the fact that Christ has put himself into their hands for all time, making them trustees of his love, and himself dependent on them.

After his resurrection, had he chosen to do so he could have revealed himself in his glory, compelling the whole world to its knees in adoration and awe; but that was not his plan. He chose to hide his glory in the lives of men, just as he had hidden it in his infancy in Bethlehem, in his boyhood as an artisan in Nazareth, in the temptations of his youth in the wilderness, in the weariness, loneliness and necessities of his manhood and, above all, in the dereliction of his passion.

It was not only of his historical passion that he spoke when he said, 'Lay up in your hearts these words; for it shall come to pass, that the son of man shall be delivered into the hands of men'. For as long as this world lasts, and men live and love and suffer and die in it, the passion of Christ will go on, and he will suffer it in the lives of men. Because this is so, all vocations, however varied outwardly, have fundamentally the same object, the comforting of Christ, and there is none of which this more true than that of caring for the mentally ill.

This is a vocation in which everyone, not only the specialist, has some part because it depends on an attitude of mind and heart, which for the majority of people must mean a change of mind and heart toward the mental sufferer, who is of all suffering people the least understood. This change of heart, and with it power to help the mental sufferer, means learning to recognise Christ in the patient, and to recognise the patient's own vocation, his part in Christ's passion and his gift to the world. For he, by his unique suffering, is taking part in the world's redemption.

This must never be forgotten. The mental sufferer must never be regarded as one whose life is without purpose or meaning, as a burden to his family, or as one who gives nothing to those who care for him, because he is in fact giving the redeeming suffering of Christ, on which the salvation of the world and each one of us depends.

It may be objected that the suffering of a mentally ill person cannot be called a vocation, or a real taking part in the passion, because he has not chosen it, and usually he is not even reconciled to it. It is precisely because that is so that those who wish to help him must realise it, and be able to explain his tragedy to him in its true light, the light of his part in Christ's body on earth, in order that he may be able not to choose but to accept his suffering, and to realise himself as one who is in the deepest communion with others because he is at the very heart of the passion, the central point in the mind of the suffering Christ, from which mercy stems and flowers. Christ as man, and he was really man, did not choose his passion, he accepted it: 'My Father, if it is possible let this chalice pass me by; only as thy will is, not as mine is'.

Long ago all mental illness was simply regarded as being diabolical possession. Roughly a hundred years ago those who were mentally ill were regarded and treated as criminals, and at that time criminals were not even treated as human beings.

In the hospitals, then so wrongly called 'asylums', only the lowest types consented to act as attendants. The patients, or prisoners as they really were, were not given treatment or nursing, but punishment. They were put into heavily weighted strait-jackets, making it impossible for them to lift their hands. They were beaten and half starved, they were often left in solitary confinement and in space so constricted that they could neither stand up nor lie down straight. They were given fetid water to drink, and no sanitary arrangements at all.

This was at the peak of Protestantism in England, when the patients were put into cages on Sundays (when their keepers did no work) without food or water at all, and there exposed to the passers-by, usually pious ladies who amused themselves on their way home from church by poking them through the bars with their parasols!

Today the attitude of the specialists has swung round completely and touches the other extreme. Whereas in the past the patient was treated as if he were guilty, the tendency among modern psychiatrists is to treat him as if he is soulless, and so incapable of moral guilt. But in the minds of most of the laity there still lingers an instinctive feeling that mental illness carries a stigma—would that they would recognise it as Christ's stigmata!

Modern treatments, drugs and surgery, have put a power into the hands of doctors and psychiatrists which, when it is used by those who are without faith, is frightening because those who are without faith cannot really know what a human being is, they cannot know that he is soul and body, let alone that he is 'another Christ'.

The majority of doctors and psychiatrists are unbelievers, often selflessly dedicated to their work of attempting to heal the mind, yet acting more in the darkness than the patient himself, because they do not know what a man is or can become. And it is into their hands that the sufferers have been delivered as never before, now not only their bodies but their souls, or at all events the three powers of their souls— their memory, their understanding and their will.

I do not think it unjust or fantastic to say that only christians who know Christ in the sufferer can ever make the new methods of treating them creative, or can be safe in using them, even when it seems imperative to do so. Equally I believe that only nurses and others who realise that the care of the mentally ill is a contemplative vocation, an entering into Christ's passion through compassion, can hope to bring even the little alleviation and momentary relief which is sometimes all that can be given to a tormented mind.

There are two main reasons for this. The first applies to all, but most of all to the doctors and research workers: only that reverence for human nature which comes from knowing that it is indwelt by God can make a helpless mental invalid safe in another man's hands. Secondly, and this is perhaps especially for those who nurse the mentally ill in hospitals or at home: only the Christ-love in their own souls, and a steady concentration on Christ hidden by the disfigurements of suffering, can give them the unfailing patience and perseverance through which, and through which alone, their work can become blessed and even creative. Without this Christ-love, without this vision of faith, they will become 'case-hardened' and hardened altogether; they will fall into depression themselves, and even come to hate those whom they can serve only through love.

What is the very special part in Christ's redeeming passion which the mentally ill are privileged to play? Outwardly it is not easy to recognise it—at first. There are some people who are even scandalised by the suggestion; they point out that the symptoms of mental illness really seem more diabolical than anything else, certainly they lack the calm, sweetness and majesty of Christ. The fantasies of the insane, and even of the unbalanced, are in extreme cases obscene, so also is their language—in fact their critics have a sneaking belief in both Freud and the idea of possession by the Devil, hopelessly irreconcilable though those two schools of thought are with each other!

I think that mental sufferers are reliving all through the ages two of Christ's experiences: his temptation in the wilderness and his agony in Gethsemane. Satan can press upon the mind and find a way into the soul, invade every sense and thought. Christ himself was really tempted, and tempted to just those things that haunt and delude people in certain kinds of insanity—to put the needs of the body (and I say *needs* deliberately) before those of the soul; to make themselves equal to God, or claim special supernatural rights and privileges; and grandiosity, to be Lords of the world. These are the most common ideas that press upon mental sufferers, and present themselves to them persistently in hallucinations and 'voices'.

But these were the ideas presented to Christ by Satan in the wilderness. Moreover not only did Christ deliver himself into the hands of men, he also, incredible though it seems, allowed Satan in some mysterious way to handle him! 'Next the Devil took him into the holy city, and there set him down on the pinnacle of the temple'.

Now we come to Gethsemane, and here Christ came close to despair, here he suffered the fear, the feeling of guilt, the dread, that is common to those who are mentally ill. 'And now he grew sorrowful and dismayed. My soul, he said, is ready to die with sorrow'.

But how are we to make the neurotic and the mentally ill see their identification with Christ without giving them a new source of hallucination and rationalisation of their conduct? This does indeed raise an interesting and a very practical question, or rather host of questions.

First, in this it is very important to distinguish between those who *are* mentally ill, or insane, and those who are really neurotic. Mental illness is not, as so many seem to think, simply an extension of neurosis; although in some of its forms the early symptoms of insanity resemble some forms of neurosis so closely as to make an early diagnosis almost an impossibility.

Let us take those who are really insane, who usually have cycles of insanity and cycles of sanity in between. During the insane or maniacal period these poor people clearly have no responsibility morally, and simply depend on others to protect them from their madness; but during the cycles of sanity it is possible to talk to them. They are usually schizophrenic types, and most schizophrenics are the intellectual type of person and are well able to realise in sane periods the danger and absurdity of grandiosity. The first thing to do, during the sane periods, is to instil into their minds the basic human qualities of Christ's character: namely utter humility, love for men so great that he was willing to be rejected by them, and in the hour of crucifixion even to feel himself abandoned by God.

Now the patient is being asked to unite herself, during the times she can use her will, to this humble, self-effacing Christ, who is willing to let all the beauty of his humanity be hidden under the terrible ugliness of our sins. Any idea of arrogance or grandiosity is impossible in Christ, who is 'obedient even unto death'. The patient must learn that her union with Christ will deepen and strengthen each time she makes an act of will to accept the humiliation and desolation of her illness. She must learn too that in doing all she is told to do while rational to help herself—even in remaining in the hospital—she is using Christ's obedience. She must be reassured that when the attacks of mania come on the offering of her will that she has made will not lose its validity: her soul will be in God's hands then, though it will seem forsaken. And she must be further reassured that those who are looking after her will during those times be responsible to see and protect the Christ in her. Just as a mother has to be a little child's will before he comes to the age of reason, those who care for the insane must be the will of the patient when he is irrational.

Of course there are tragic cases when there is no rational period ever, and there may never have been a chance for anyone who loves God to talk to the person during the borderline period. In these cases the 'treatment' is on a really mystical plane (I don't mean the medical treatment).

The only thing to be done is for the nurse or attendant to practice acts of love and reverence to the patient so consistently and so perseveringly and with such faith that, even if they see no sign of it, the patient may—at some level that we are still unable to explore—have an occasional glimmering of realisation that he is loved: that someone has seen not the exterior that is repulsive, but something interior that attracts. Only in eternity will the full result of heroic supernatural love like that be known to us.

In the case of neurotics the idea of identification with Christ is likely to be misunderstood and seized on to their own undoing. To guard against this I think the thing to remember is: start by trying to give them an impression of what *Christ* is like, not what *they* are like; in other words, an objective and a new conception of Christ.

Undoubtedly in neurosis prevention is better and much easier than cure. I attribute the increase of neurosis in our day to the decrease of christianity in the education of children. There are what we might call not only pre-dispositions physically to neurosis, but predisposing circumstances that are certain to produce neurotics if they exist and are not treated from the start. They are well known: circumstances which cause a child to feel humiliated, overlooked or self-conscious either at home or at school. Now only if the child can be taught gently to know the humility of the Christ-child, how he was unnoticed, how he was slighted on earth, can he begin to find out for himself that in sharing Christ's experience he is being honoured. I say let him work it out for himself. Except in rare cases it would be a mistake to tell a child, 'You are sharing Christ's humiliation'. This would probably give him a fearful pose of martyrdom and isolation. But he must learn what Christ's values are, that Christ indwells us all, and in each one his indwelling is lived out in a different way; he must grow up growing in the knowledge that the indwelling of Christ is a communion between us all. A Jewish psychiatrist said to me once: 'Where there is the humility of Christ from the start, there can be no psychological scars'.

It is important to get a neurotic to understand that our identification with Christ is something we all share with one another, that each of us (as a rule) individually lives out only one aspect of Christ's life at a time, and to try to discover which that is in his individual case. If the neurotic's tendency is simply to declare his own preposterous behaviour as 'God's will' and beyond his control, and indeed a cause for personal aggrandisement, it is well to tell him quite simply that if indeed he has no responsibility for his actions he should be certified as a lunatic, and that what God wills for him is not that he should make himself a nuisance. He should discover which of Christ's *real* characteristics he is asked to cultivate; usually it will be his obedience, perhaps his beautiful humility in accepting himself as a normal, even ordinary, human being, subject to ordinary needs like eating and sleeping. The pitfall is when a neurotic tries not to unite himself to Christ through overcoming temptations of vanity and resentment associated with and aggravated by his neurosis, but to dramatise himself (and that, did he realise it, blasphemously) by trying even to dramatise the Christ in him!

Take the example, so common, of neurotics who insist upon self-starvation, who pretend they have no desire to eat—which after some years may well be true. They must be made to see that the Christ in them is the ordinary human Christ who made himself as man dependent on food, who always concerned himself to see that his apostles had it even when he had risen from the dead, who in fact ate when he really need not have in his glorified body, who had it put on record forever that when he did fast he got hungry and was tempted to turn stones to bread—unlike the neurotic who would like to turn bread to stone. These people must stop meditating on emaciated, imaginary conceptions of Christ, and make their prayer every mouthful of food they eat, and every hour of sleep they invite, their prayer of realisation of Christ's simplicity and of Christ's reality in them. How hard a pill it is to swallow that one's own particular Christhood is the ordinariness and not the extraordinariness of Christ. It unites one with one's fellow men.

Mental patients often live out their lives in Gethsemane, and without alleviation for the fear and conflict that they suffer—and here it is that we discover the very core of the vocation of those who serve them. It is compassion. Perhaps there is nothing harder to sustain than compassion with those who cannot be cured.

People inflamed with apostolic zeal are ready enough to work for results, to see a sick person recover and a sinner repent, to alleviate poverty, to teach one who is ignorant; anything that shows results is stimulating, and it can be almost dangerously satisfying! But the poor neurotic who always seems to relapse, or the insane person pronounced incurable (though in these days that word has almost lost its meaning)—these people do not show results—there is no satisfaction waiting for those who serve them!

Their great need is that which Christ pleaded for in Gethsemane—compassion. He did not ask them to try to do away with his anguish or to alleviate his passion, but simply to be with him, to enter into his suffering through compassion. But this even Peter, who would so gladly have swept the passion away, could not do! 'Then he went back to his disciples to find them asleep; and he said to Peter, had you no strength then to watch with me even for an hour?'

It is the same today. In the mental sufferer Christ asks first of all and most of all for compassion, for those who will simply be with him, who will see through the sweat of his agony to the secret of his love.

It is significant that on those two occasions of profound mental stress Christ was unable to regain his strength and peace alone. As man he was not self-sufficient, he accepted human limitations, and the mental suffering he endured was too much for him to bear alone. On both occasions after the storm was spent angels sent by God came to comfort him.

The servant is not greater than the master. Christ in his members cannot endure mental torment alone; therefore it is well to pray that there will be many vocations among Catholics who have faith and vision and Christ's love to care for the mentally ill, and that they will share in the unimaginable joy of the angels who comforted Christ.

The Artist's Vocation

The Liturgical Artist and the Worker

During the war I have often asked myself this question:
'Have artists anything at all to give to humanity, in this
world as it is—not as we wish it to be, but as it is now?' This
question was a personal one for me, because in a very humble
way I am an artist myself, and therefore am obliged to
answer it from the point of view of conscience, not merely as
an interesting idea for abstract discussion.

Whatever evil war causes, it brings us one realisation that
is good; it compels us to realise that we are, each of us, part
of a whole, part of the whole of humanity, with the
responsibility of sharing in its suffering and its glory.

Faced with the peril and hardship of war, everyone who
was not a complete megalomaniac was ready, even eager, to
sink the idea of self-importance and do any job, however
seemingly insignificant, that would really serve humanity.
People no longer valued themselves by how much more
gifted they were than other people, by how exclusive their
talents made them, or by how the advantages they happened
to possess protected them from a hard lot. On the contrary
the only value was how much could one give, how could one
serve, how most be in communion with the rest of humanity.

As the problem while the war lasted was how to overcome
physical danger and hardship, we naturally tended to get
rather a materialistic conception of what service to humanity
really is, and almost forgot that this war could never have
happened, could not have happened in the way that it did,
or have left the aftermath that it has, had we not been making
this mistake for a very long time, the mistake of putting

man's natural needs far and away above his supernatural needs, his body far and away above his soul, forgetting what man really is, that he is soul and body, that he has natural and supernatural life, that he is made in the image and likeness of God.

This danger, of forgetting what man is, is even greater now than it was during the war. Then the visible uncertainty of life did help us to remember that even here and now there is another life besides the one we see.

Those who experienced the raids in which continual bombing lasted all through the hours of darkness until the brain registered only one thought, 'it will stop when the light comes', will understand what I mean by saying that the coming of morning light was a symbol of what peace would be when it came, or what we imagined that it would be, dawn filling an empty sky, a growing light in which there would be no fear of one another, in which there would be silence and the beginning of a new day.

We realised then, with every dawn, how wonderful it was to be allowed to have one's life for another day. Life—just life itself—was realised for the miracle that it is, and the mind, free in that moment from every sentiment but gratitude for life, was wholly alive and sensitive to its wonder.

In such moments, the heart does really seem like a morning sky, empty of everything but light; and in that emptiness every tiny thing that reveals the innocence of living joy stands out sharp and clear and fills us with its significance of sheer loveliness.

This is no mere sentimentality, I know of what I am speaking. I have seen the shadow of a flower in the moonlight on a London garden path while bombs were falling on London. I have heard a bird singing in the first light above the debris of my own street, and on the faces of others passing in the dawn I have seen that which has made me certain that if they could forget all the mawkish mis-representations of Christ that have obscured man's vision, and know him simply as the Son of God, who said 'I have come so that they may have life and have it more abundantly', his conquest of their love would be accomplished.

Of course everyone knew that when the war was over its terrible effects would not be over, and they would make as big, perhaps a bigger demand on us than the war itself. But at that time of purification it seemed certain that when at last it was possible to begin to rebuild the world everyone would have learnt that the simple values of Christ are the way to peace, that his life in us is the true life, and would work for that with a single heart.

As you know, that has not happened. There is no need for me to dwell on the tragedy of what is happening in the whole world now. It must be plain to everyone, who thinks at all, that now men have forgotten what a whole man is. Christ's values, simplicity, humility, poverty, gentleness, love, are not recognised as ways to happiness, or that it is man's necessity to know, love and serve God, and his greatest need of all is to adore him.

Once again, Christ is weeping over Jerusalem, the Jerusalem of New York, London and Moscow. 'Ah, if thou couldst understand above all in this day that is granted to thee, the ways that can bring thee peace! As it is they are hidden from thy sight'.

This only makes the artist want more than ever to know that he has a part in the service of humanity, that he is not merely decorating life but taking part in it, living it as one of the workers of the world in full communion with all the others and working with them for the things that bring us peace.

It seems to me that he not only has a part, but that if he is faithful to the demands of his vocation he has, after the priest, the most essential part of all. It is his responsibility to keep the true meaning and dignity of work before men's eyes, and to show to their yet more astonished eyes that work, if it is properly understood, is one of the greatest of all means to human happiness as well as to human goodness.

It is well to remember some simple facts about work which have generally been forgotten, and to correct one big mistake which may be at the root of all our other mistakes. This root mistake is that work is a punishment for sin, consequently an unhappy means of expiation. Many people think that if Adam had not sinned, there would have been no work at all. This is untrue. Before Adam sinned, he was told to work, but it was to be a joyful experience, a prayer, an immediate contact with God.

Adam was to work in the garden of Eden, in which there was only happiness and an unimaginable intimacy with God and still no shadow of sin: 'And the Lord God took the man and put him into the garden of Eden to dress it and to keep it' (Gen 2:15). Work in the garden of Eden was not the condition for living, it was simply a delight, but after Adam sinned his punishment included that work could only be done with a painful effort and it was to be the condition for his daily bread: 'In the sweat of thy face shalt thou eat bread, till thou return unto the ground' (Gen 3:19).

What then *was* work exactly, in the morning of primal innocence? A delight—but for one who knew God as sinless man knew God, there could only be one delight, however diverse its forms. It could only be closer union with God.

Work then was a prayer, not in the sense simply of being a hard thing 'offered up' in a penitent spirit, but contemplation, in which man discovered the image and likeness of God in himself. Without it man was not complete, for it crowned his happiness, and this may be a reason why even today we feel an instinctive pity for those who do not work.

It is true that now, because of sin, work is not the unhampered union with God that it was before the fall, but by living a workman's life himself Christ has taken the sting out of Adam's humiliation, and made the sweat of his face his glory. And through work modern man can, if he will, still restore God's image and likeness in himself, and begin the contemplation of the Trinity in the mirror of his own heart.

It is at this point that the artist's work for the world begins. It is he who alone holds fast to the ideal of *good work* before all else, who delights in the work itself for its own sake, and is ready to put aside not only riches, but comfort and what others think necessities for it. By his fidelity he keeps that ideal before men's eyes. His values are the pure values of a child, which open the kingdom of heaven to him. Here and now his motive is disinterested love.

Every man living has buried, somewhere within him, the instinct to make his own image and likeness, to make *something* that has the qualities of goodness and truth that every man believes to be in his soul. In the making he could learn something from his own heart of the utter joy and love operating in the blessed Trinity in making him.

Artists are often tiresome people, but the world extends an amazing charity to them, perhaps because everyone is secretly hiding, and often denying, an artist in himself. There is always a response to the work of a man's hands. Children stand absorbed for hours watching a craftsman at work. Tough soldiers stand enchanted round a toy-maker in the camp. The work of art has always been the thing which has distinguished man as human, from the time he lived in the cave until now. If the worker fostered the artist in his heart he would make work human today.

Christ has hallowed the effort in work, so that which was part of our punishment is now turned to our good, and in the acquiring of skill, in itself arduous, the craftsman both expiates the world's sin and integrates his own being.

The young apprentice not yet conditioned to his job is astonished at his own clumsiness, at how long it takes him and how much perseverance to develop the delicacy, together with the strength, necessary to a craftsman's hands, the patience to acquire an exact eye, and how much repeated exercise of self-discipline to coordinate mind and body into the harmony, as exact and melodious as pure music, which is the minimum demand of a craftsman's skill.

I remember an old cobbler in a back street in Lisbon making a little pair of red leather shoes, with Spanish heels, and rejoicing because there was still a dancing foot in the world, small enough and shapely enough for the perfection of his skill. He took the finely turned heel into his gnarled old hand and his fingers closed on it like a caress: 'Eight hours every day for thirty years has gone into the making of that heel' he said.

Unhappily very few of the multitude of workers seem to have that spirit today. Machinery, industry, economic conditions seem to be stronger than humanity in men, but only seem to be. We could begin to destroy the illusion of the power of these things over the human spirit by being careful in our speech. Have we not for example given machinery an almost uncanny atmosphere in the people's mind by invariably speaking of it in pompous articles as 'the Machine'? 'The Machine' conjures up an impression of a demoniacal false God, but machines, with a small 'm' and in the plural are playthings for men and boys.

I do not believe that there is any hope of our knowing the things that are to our peace until the worker gets back the secret of contemplation through his work, and this he will only do when he wants to with his whole will. When a worker does want something with his whole will he gets it. We know how men set about getting more wages, shorter hours, better conditions; even 'the Machine' does not prevent them, but whoever heard of a man standing out for the sheer goodness of his work, his integrity as a man or the likeness of God in his soul.

It is the apostolate of the artist to inspire in the worker that longing and the will to achieve it. When a child has been watching a craftsman for a while he is certain to say 'Let me do it'. The artist's job is to waken the child in the working man to the same longing and the same insistence.

In this way the artist is a reformer, but the liturgical artist is more than a reformer. He is to the ordinary worker what the cloistered contemplative is to the layman.

The contemplative is the will of Christ on earth, in him all the hesitating desires and fragmentary oblations of the world are offered once and for all to God. He is the Christ-will of the mystical body, in him the broken world is whole. In the liturgical artist all that is good in all the work of all the workers of the world, and all their skill and their labour is concentrated and offered consciously as prayer. In him the work of all workers is restored to its primal innocence and joy.

The liturgical artist is not out to express himself, he is out to express the mind of the church, to bring the offerings of men to the foot of the altar. He shares in and expresses the humility and anonymity of countless workers who for their part share in the humility of Christ at Nazareth. During his twenty-odd years as a carpenter, he must have made hundreds of things superbly, but not one of his works has ever been preserved or was in his own time even known of. For that matter his works are in front of our eyes today but seldom recognised. How seldom do we catch our breath for wonder and love when we look up at the milky way or down at the multitudinous grass.

The liturgical artist goes on making vestments and vessels for the altar in the shape of the church's design, always aiming at what is true to her mind, at what is simpler and purer, never at self-expression or originality. His offering is not better than that of other men because beautiful things ultimately flower from his finger tips, but is the offering of other men, the symbol of all the work of Christ in the worker.

The liturgy is the prayer of Christ on earth. Incorporated into it is another universal prayer that belongs to all men and to Christ in all men; this is the prayer of the body.

Our Lord began this prayer when his little new body shivered, at the first kiss of our cold midnight. He offered it in Joseph's workroom, in the sweat of his face and the flow of his muscles, in the sawing and planing of the wood, in eating and drinking and sleeping, in hungering and fasting in the wilderness, in the physical ardours and endurances of his public life, in the breaking of the bread at the last supper, in the bruising and scourging of his trial, in his nakedness on Calvary, in the stretching out of his hands and feet to the nails, in his thirst and the drying of his flesh and his dying on the cross, in his lying dead in the tomb and the raising of his body from the dead, in his ascending in his body to his Father with the five wounds blazing on it like five stars.

In Christ in man the prayer goes on—in the humility of the littleness of children, in the suffering and patience of invalids, in the hardships and fatigues of soldiers, in the hunger and thirst and nakedness of the persecuted, in the patience of pregnant women, in the dependence of old people and in the weakness of the dying. It can be offered too in the joys of the body, in the strength and well-being of the young, in the grateful enjoyment of food and drink and sleep, in the sweetness of hallowed love and the splendour of consecrated passion, and superbly in the dedication of hands and eyes and muscle and sinew of the liturgical artist.

All that applies to the ordinary artist concerning the getting and keeping of skill applies even more to the artist who works for the sanctuary. We can look out over the working world and see the ascending scale of beauty from the first struggle of the apprentice with the clumsiness of his hands to the lifting up of the chalice in the anointed hands of the priest.

The liturgy is the prayer of Christ in his church, and his church is every christian. In the liturgy every aspiration, every desire, every work of every christian is gathered and transformed. His darkness is flooded with light, his secret and formless longing takes shape and becomes visible, his inarticulate praise is audible. His whole being is unified in the beauty of adoration. A law of ultimate beauty imposes a pattern of restraint on his emotions, which lifts them up from the dust whence he comes into the light of eternal life. In the voice of the priest the Christ-voice of the dumb love of the earth is heard in heaven.

The liturgical artist clothes man's prayer in beauty. He vests Christ in man for the sacrifice. He shows the world its own joys and sorrows when Christ has put them on. His mourning vested in black, his suffering in crimson, his hope in the colour of the green leaf, his contrition royally in purple, and the joy and resurrection of his heart in the whiteness of the blossom of the tree.

He hands the wine of humanity to the priest, in the cup of beaten gold that is the symbol of the work of all men's hands in his. There his work ends and the prayer of Christ on earth is taken up, and offered by the priest, in whom both worker and artist are present and are lifted up.

In the priest at the altar, the glory of humanity is achieved by Christ. The prayer of the body is manifest in the trained and ordered movements of worship, restrained and intensified by the austere technique and musical law of the liturgy. Here in the fasting of the celebrant is the world's hunger and thirst, in the bowing down and beating of the breast the humility of all the world's suffering, in the raising, opening and extending of the priest's hands all joy that lifts and opens the hearts of men, in the arms extended wide in the form of the cross all the world's charity.

We have come a long way from the first fumbling of the hands of the apprentice, learning to strike true with his wooden mallet, to the hands of the priest at the altar, moving swiftly to the climax of love in the identical movements and gestures of 'the holy and venerable hands' of Christ our Lord at the last supper.

Now I have answered my question, whether artists have anything at all to give to humanity in this world as it is today. I have at all events answered my own conscience. The artist restores the real meaning of work as contemplation.

The liturgical artist gives a chalice beaten out from his own life, in which the hearts of all the workers and all the world are to be consecrated in the heart of Christ. 'Sentence is now being passed on this world: Now is the time when the prince of this world is to be cast out. Yes, if only I am lifted up from the earth, I will attract all men to myself.' (Jn 12:31–32).

Why I Like It

Everyone has heard said over and over again: 'I don't know why I like a thing, but I do know what I like'. The odd thing is that this useless remark is never uttered shamefacedly; it is usually spoken with vague defiance, as if it were a protest against the other people who do know why they like this picture or that statue; sometimes it is spoken with an unmistakable air of superiority. For convenience we will call all who make this boast 'philistines'. I do not think that they are altogether what is generally understood by this word; but they are the sort of people who are inclined to be proud of being taken for philistines: as if the lack of any working knowledge about art showed them to be healthy-minded. I do not believe that anyone really wishes to be thought a philistine. I do not believe that anyone who thinks at all, even in the obscurest way, about art, honestly thinks himself inartistic or wanting in taste.

But I do believe that many people persuade themselves that they have an inborn intuition for the good or the bad in art which excuses them from taking the trouble to educate themselves in such matters; they think their intuitions so sound that their liking a thing or not proves that it is good or bad in itself! Thus if they have glanced at a photograph of Epstein's Rima, and failed to like it, that actually proves that Epstein's Rima is not a work of art. No, if we are unwilling to take the trouble to educate our minds about art, we must give up the illusion that our taste is infallible. There may be a great deal to excuse us; we may have been either miseducated or not educated in this matter at school, and be reluctant to admit that we have to begin at the beginning and learn; we may have been put off by the affectation of many who pose as artistic, and by the long and usually meaningless names which some critics give to quite simple (but often indefinable) things in art, and have decided that the study of art is altogether beyond us; we may have no time to go to exhibitions of contemporary art because we fritter away our time in picture houses; and no time, for similar reasons, to read any books about art.

The truth of the whole matter is that we need to be educated, that we can educate ourselves, and we ought to educate ourselves in matters of art because it is one of the great sources of true joy in life. How, then, am I to educate myself? First I must get rid of all my prejudices and no longer think that the first or last 'style' in art is the only one to take seriously, or indeed that any of them are to be taken too seriously. I can begin by looking at all kinds of pictures and sculpture, ancient and modern, as if I had never seen any of them before; that will ensure my thinking about them and not taking them for granted. I can go, all alone, to exhibitions (to modern exhibitions and to museums), and without a catalogue so as to look at things not knowing who made them. I must not spend, at first, too long at this, nor attempt much on one day; but when something arrests me I must look at it for a very long time and try to learn all I can by just looking at it, until it shows me why I like it.

The next stage will be to carry a notebook and pencil. Write down the number of the work you like, and under the number why you like it. Buy a catalogue, but do not read it yet; when your notebook is full you may look up your catalogues to find out whose works you like. You will find this great fun; and you will probably discover that what you like in, say, an early Assyrian carving is the same thing that you like in the work of some almost unknown modern painter. If you make a discovery of that kind real progress has begun. But be sure you make your notes honestly, and avoid vagueness. If you like the way hair is done on a statue put that down and nothing else; perhaps you will find later on that leaves were done with the same or nearly the same strokes a thousand years earlier or later.

After you have done this sort of thing for some time you can begin to read about art. You will find a good deal of nonsense in most books on the subject, and that they frequently contradict one another; but some of them are illuminating and most of them are provocative, and it is a good thing to be provoked by a book about art. You may even write notes on your reading, especially notes contradicting the author and giving reasons for your disagreement.

If you persevere on these lines you will find that you like totally different, and many more things, than you used to like; finding in them good qualities which are at present without meaning to you. You will still prefer some things to others; but you will know *why* you prefer them; and your reasons will be based on something much better than 'intuition'. Also you will be much slower to condemn works you do not like, and to say that they are bad in themselves. And the reasons you will have for your likes will increase your enjoyment of them beyond belief. What is much more, you will begin to see beauty in the commonest things of your daily experience far more keenly: such things as a scaffolding against the sky, or your dog running.

There will be other and more general results. Being more capable of delight you will contribute more to the delight of others. You will have a fund of joy which cannot fail when material things fail. You will have become one of the few (alas!) who, having learnt to think about what they like, know *why* they like what is good.

Lightning Source UK Ltd.
Milton Keynes UK
01 July 2010

156345UK00002B/11/P